THE SALON DORÉ
from the
HÔTEL DE LA TRÉMOILLE

THE SALON DORÉ
FROM THE
HÔTEL DE LA TRÉMOILLE

MARTIN CHAPMAN

with

Alexandre Pradère

Xavier Bonnet

Lesley Bone

Maria Santangelo

FINE ARTS MUSEUMS OF SAN FRANCISCO

*This book is dedicated to
Adolphus Andrews Jr.*

Contents

Foreword ix
COLIN B. BAILEY

Donors to the Renovation
of the Salon Doré xi

Introduction
MARTIN CHAPMAN
1

History of the Salon
MARTIN CHAPMAN
17

Life in the Salon
ALEXANDRE PRADÈRE
35

*The Furnishings of the
Hôtel de La Trémoille*
XAVIER BONNET
49

A Note on the Upholstery
XAVIER BONNET
69

Conservation of the Boiserie
LESLEY BONE
77

The 1790 Inventory of the Salon 97   Gallery 100   Checklist 102

Timeline 112   Selected Bibliography 116

Acknowledgments 117   About the Contributors 119   Index 120

Foreword

The Salon Doré from the Hôtel de La Trémoille is one of the most cherished spaces in the Legion of Honor. Restored to its former glory as a *salon de compagnie*, with its gilded paneling and full complement of furnishings, it now not only represents the high point of interior decoration in late-eighteenth-century France, but also is an example of how the period room can be displayed in a more engaging manner in the twenty-first century. Recent research has revealed that the room boasts a remarkable connection to our museum: it was built originally for the duchesse de La Trémoille, whose brother commissioned the famous Hôtel de Salm in Paris, upon which the architecture of the Legion is modeled. We can imagine the two families visiting each other in our Salon, which now appears very much as it did in the 1780s.

The original purpose of renovating the Salon Doré was the restoration of its beautiful gilded paneling as a fine example of French Neoclassical architecture. The superlative design and carving of the various elements—the mirrors with their crowning trophies of the arts, the grand Corinthian pilasters, the door frames decorated with plaster overdoors modeled in low and high relief—required extensive conservation to improve their sculptural details and gilding. The larger ambition of this project took us beyond any previous reinstallation of this sort. Our aim was to furnish the room in the manner of the late eighteenth century—as a *salon de compagnie*, with the range of chairs and console tables that were characteristic of the Parisian aristocratic salon. The arrangement of the many armchairs and side chairs clarifies the decorative relationship between seat furniture and paneling, but it also tells us much more about the social history of these salons. Through this project we have been able to pare back time to glimpse the vanished conventions of *ancien régime* Paris.

Using the *hôtel*'s inventory of 1790, recently discovered by Xavier Bonnet in the Archives Nationales, Paris, we have re-created much of the Salon's appearance at that date, including the blue color scheme of the upholstery, gray paint on the walls, and the arrangement of the seating furniture. Although we do not possess the original chairs, which were lost during the French Revolution, we have reconstituted as many examples as possible of the appropriate date, style, and quality. Now twenty-one seats, including the sofa, take the place of the twenty-five items inventoried. Along with works in our permanent collection—the chandelier, the wall lights, two consoles, the clock, and the garniture of three vases on the chimneypiece—we have largely reconstructed our Salon to replicate its appearance in those halcyon days of the 1780s.

This project could not have happened without the support of the Fine Arts Museums' community. Under the leadership of Adolphus Andrews Jr., substantial funds were raised to run this endeavor, which is now named for Cynthia Fry Gunn and John A. Gunn, who are the principal donors. I thank the Gunns, Fine Arts Museums president of the Board of Trustees Diane B. Wilsey, members of the European Decorative Arts Council (EDAC), and others from our city who have so generously supported this renovation. We are immensely grateful to Breguet as the corporate sponsor of this undertaking. I further extend gratitude to EDAC member Andrew Skurman, of Andrew Skurman Architects, who, with his staff, donated his design services to this project. Benjamin Steinitz of Galerie Steinitz in Paris gave a parquet floor and also provided much advice and assistance, running the aspects of the conservation project in the French capital. Xavier Bonnet of Atelier Saint-Louis, Paris, not only unveiled the inventory, but also researched the silk that was used at the Hôtel de La Trémoille and provided the historically accurate new upholstery, and he communicated his findings in two essays written for this catalogue. Alexandre Pradère wrote a fascinating account of life in the salons, which also can be found in these pages. This book is published with the generous assistance of EDAC and the Andrew W. Mellon Foundation Endowment for Publications.

I also wish to thank those who have contributed to bringing this Salon to fruition: notably, Martin Chapman, curator in charge of European decorative arts and sculpture, who initiated this project; Maria Santangelo, associate curator of European decorative arts and sculpture, who managed so much of it; Patricia Lacson, director of facilities, who oversaw the construction; and Lesley Bone, objects conservator, who led the restoration so ably. Lesley Bone also conceived the building of a temporary conservation studio with a large window where our visitors have enjoyed watching the progress of work on the paneling over the past fifteen months.

COLIN B. BAILEY
Director of Museums
Fine Arts Museums
of San Francisco

Donors to the Renovation of the Salon Doré

Major Patrons
Cynthia Fry Gunn and John A. Gunn
in memory of John E. Buchanan, Jr.

Corporate Sponsor
Breguet

Patrons

Jamie and Philip Bowles
Ray and Dagmar Dolby Family Fund
Mr. and Mrs. Staffan Encrantz
The European Decorative Arts Council
The Fifth Age of Man Foundation
Mr. and Mrs. Richard W. Goss II
F. Scott Gross and Terry S. Gross

Mr. and Mrs. William Hamilton
Samuel H. Kress Foundation
Françoise and Andrew Skurman
Mr. Benjamin Steinitz
in memory of Bernard B. Steinitz
The Michael Taylor Trust
Diane B. Wilsey

Patron Gifts in Memory of John E. Buchanan, Jr.

Mr. and Mrs. Adolphus Andrews Jr.
The Kimball Foundation
Jeannik Méquet Littlefield
Denise Littlefield Sobel

Mr. and Mrs. Bernard Osher
Constance Crowley Peabody
Lonna Wais

INTRODUCTION

Martin Chapman

Many people love period rooms. They can provide some of the most engaging displays in museums by combining fine examples of interior architecture with corresponding pieces of furniture and decorative arts. When thoughtfully installed, they can evoke cogent impressions of life in eras past and provide lessons in the history of design and architecture. In recent decades, however, period rooms have nearly vanished from American museums. The minimalist aesthetic agenda, which has been the favored mode of museum architecture since the 1980s, is one reason for this decline. Shifts in cultural ideology also have contributed to their disappearance—to the extent that even the term "period room" has occasionally become one of opprobrium in museology. In this book, "period room" is employed without apology because it is, at its best, one of the most evocative types of display conceived for the art museum.

The de Young museum in San Francisco is a prime example of the trend of moving away from period rooms in the past thirty years. Although the old de Young in the second half of the twentieth century contained as many as sixteen such rooms, when the new building opened in 2005, none were included in its galleries.[1] Admittedly, there were often good reasons for dismissing period rooms. Questions about the authenticity of architectural elements were common, and problems of relating objects to each other within a room could seem insurmountable. Sometimes period rooms simply went stale as they aged poorly over the years. Museum curators and directors started to veer away from such displays. In the 1970s, officials at London's Victoria and Albert Museum doubted the wisdom of showing so many period rooms, arguing that more authentic interiors could be readily seen in the many British country houses that were open to the public. Several rooms were thus removed from view, initiating a process that was followed in other museums.

Some museums, however, held faith in the period room because it was seen as an important

FIG. 1. The Grand Salon from the Hôtel de Tessé, Paris, ca. 1768–1772, with later additions. Made by Nicolas Huyot (French, 1700–1791) and carved by Pierre Fixon (French, active 1748–1788) and/or his son Louis-Pierre Fixon (French, b. 1748). Metropolitan Museum of Art, New York, gift of Mrs. Herbert N. Straus, 1942, 42.203.1. This *boiserie*, with its arched mirrors surmounted by trophies and the same model of plaster overdoor by Fixon, is very similar in design to the Legion's Salon Doré. The Tessé room was in fact a *salle du dais*, or audience chamber.

part of the entity's cultural program. The Philadelphia Museum of Art, which under the historian of the rococo Fiske Kimball (1888–1955) in the 1920s and 1930s had initiated an articulated fabric of historic interiors balanced between galleries of paintings and sculptures, has remained the shining example of how the period room can be successfully integrated into an institutional setting. The much-loved Wrightsman rooms at the Metropolitan Museum of Art in New York were completely refurbished in the early 2000s, with a fresh agenda based on the times of the day (see fig. 1). The American wing in the same museum has undergone a reinstallation of its rooms more recently, and the J. Paul Getty Museum, Los Angeles, incorporated a suite of French rooms—renamed "paneled rooms"—into its displays when the new Brentwood site opened in 1997. In the late 1990s, the Victoria and Albert Museum also rethought its period rooms when it reinstalled its British galleries with the finest of its interiors reconfigured to reflect modern research by eliminating later additions and restoring lost sections to return them to their original footprints, such as the Norfolk House Music Room (fig. 2). In the early twenty-first century, it seems that the pendulum has begun to swing the other way, and museums with longer-term perspectives have recognized that the period room can be a valuable part of an institution's mission and display. With deeper research and a more vibrant approach, the period room—previously deemed fusty—can be transformed into an exceptional tool for understanding the past.

Today the Legion of Honor incorporates three period rooms in its displays (plus a ceiling from a Spanish palace in Toledo), which were included in the reinstallations of the 1990s. This situation

FIG. 2. The Music Room from Norfolk House, London, 1748–1756. Designed by Matthew Brettingham the Elder (English, 1699–1769) and decorated by Giovanni Battista Borra (Italian, 1713–1770). Victoria and Albert Museum, London. The recent reinstallation of this room re-created the window wall. Although it has no furniture, the room has an atmosphere that has been recaptured by lighting from the wall sconces.

is the diametric opposite of what occurred in the past at the Fine Arts Museums. While the de Young had actively pursued its program of rooms throughout the postwar era, the Legion had no examples of them until the late 1950s, when it was offered a fine French eighteenth-century suite of paneling. What is now identified as the *boiserie* (paneling) from the Salon Doré of the Hôtel de La Trémoille is the finest of all the rooms acquired by the two museums that today compose the Fine Arts Museums of San Francisco.

Mr. and Mrs. Richard Rheem donated the paneling in 1959, and the director of the Legion of Honor at the time, Thomas Carr Howe, recognized it as a worthwhile addition to the museum. The impressive Neoclassical style of this French *boiserie*, which is articulated by gilded Corinthian pilasters set between arched mirrors topped by trophies, represents the best of French eighteenth-century interior architecture in terms of design and craftsmanship. Howe must have been impressed that the paneling also reflected the Neoclassical style of the museum, which is modeled on the Hôtel de Salm in Paris (today the Palais de la Légion d'Honneur; see fig. 40). Since then, however, the Salon of the Hôtel de La Trémoille has been found to have a much closer relationship with the Hôtel de Salm than anyone realized—as will be discussed in "History of the Salon" in this volume.

CONCEIVING A NEW FUTURE FOR THE SALON

The fine quality of the carving and the fluency of the design alone merited rethinking the installation of this *boiserie* in recent years, but there was much more to consider in reinterpreting this Salon—and in making it fresh and vibrant for modern visitors. The architectural historian John Harris has stated that the Salon is one of the four finest French period rooms in an American museum.[2] Shown initially as a conventional period room in the early 1960s after it was first installed at the Legion, the Salon had a more or less historically accurate ceiling, parquet floor, actual windows, curtains, and a scattering of fine furniture from the room's era (see fig. 8). It was dismantled when the museum was retrofitted for seismic protection in the early 1990s.

Moved to a new space in the museum after the renovation, the Salon was designated a "paneled environment" rather than a "period room," which at the time had seemed an outmoded term.

There it served as a background for a study display of furniture arranged on platforms. The parquet floor and ceiling were omitted, and in their place the existing museum floor and ceiling were used, and the windows were turned into lighted glass showcases (see fig. 3). This minimalist approach was in concert with the museum's larger program of renovation, but it lacked luster. Therefore, museum curators and staff considered a new vision of how to display this important room.

RESEARCH LEADING TO A NEW DESIGN FOR THE ROOM

The main philosophy behind the new display of the Salon was to use historical research from as far back as possible to inform a fresh interpretation. Tracing the story of the Salon along a trail of bread crumbs left by the expert on French rooms Bruno Pons (1954–1995) resulted in the room's *boiserie* acquiring a much earlier provenance. Since the 1960s, the Salon had been thought to come from the great aristocratic town house the Hôtel d'Humières (see fig. 4), on rue de Lille in Paris, which was demolished in 1905. It was one of the many private mansions, called *hôtels particuliers*, built on the Left Bank in the early eighteenth century. In the end this provenance for the paneling turned out to be true only for the years between 1879 and 1905, but Pons established that the *boiserie* previously had decorated another vanished Parisian *hôtel particulier*, the Hôtel de La Trémoille on rue Saint-Dominique, which was torn down in the 1870s as a result of the construction of the boulevard Saint-Germain under the Haussmann Plan for rebuilding Paris.

Pons published papers verifying that the architect Pierre-Auguste Delapoize (?–1799) installed

FIG. 3. The Salon Doré in its 1995 installation at the Legion of Honor, with the lighted glass cabinets at right. The paneling was installed in the existing shell of the gallery, retaining the museum's parquet floor and ceiling, with spotlights and lighted showcases added.

the *boiserie* of "a Salon Doré" in the Hôtel de La Trémoille in 1781.[3] This documentation gave historians much earlier evidence of the room as well as its name—and it altered the room's history significantly. The *boiserie* is believed to have been installed in the Hôtel de La Trémoille from 1781 to 1877—a much longer period than the twenty-six or so years during which it ornamented the Salon in the Hôtel d'Humières—and therefore its name has been changed to reflect its earlier setting. The La Trémoilles were one of the oldest families of France, and the duke and duchess installed the handsome *boiserie* at the time of the marriage of their eldest son, the prince de Tarente, to his bride, mademoiselle de Châtillon, an heiress who inherited the house from her father, the duc du Châtillon. (For more on the La Trémoille family, see "History of the Salon" in this volume.)

With this earlier provenance uncovered, research no longer concentrated on the Hôtel d'Humières. The surviving plans of the Hôtel de La Trémoille provided new evidence about the original layout of the room. Rather than the rectangular shape of the 1990s Legion installation, the room was originally square, or close to square.[4] The plans confirmed what Pons wrote in his book on French period rooms: square was the conventional form of the Parisian aristocratic salon, particularly in the early eighteenth century.[5] Changing the room back to its original square

FIG. 4. The Salon Doré installed at the Hôtel d'Humières, Paris, ca. 1905. The *boiserie* was extended to fit the larger dimensions of the d'Humières salon but preserved its original square floor plan. The room was furnished with much overstuffed and tufted seat furniture and a thick carpet typical of the late nineteenth century.

plan shifts the proportions of the walls so that the main architectural elements—the grand Corinthian pilasters, the mirrors with their trophies, and the door cases—are balanced and the room is articulated by a more regular rhythm of pilasters, as if inside a Roman temple. This effect likely would have been the aim of the architect, Delapoize, and it would be essential for the successful renovation of the room.

The next aspect was to reinstate the missing elements of the room, according to eighteenth-century architectural principles, in order to re-create its original form. The Salon had been altered in its many installations, such as that in the Otto Kahn mansion at 1 East 91st Street in New York, where it was moved in 1918 and where one mirror was removed to make an extra doorway (see fig. 13). The tall windows, for example, which were eliminated in the 1990s in favor of showcases, were restored, along with a ceiling based on eighteenth-century precedents, the parquet floor, and two sets of doors. Rather than being cluttered with air-conditioning registers and spotlights, the ceiling is now plain and relieved by a gilded rosette in the center, from which the chandelier is suspended. The San Francisco architect Andrew Skurman donated his services to help design the new structure for the room and its architectural details, and the Parisian antiques dealer Benjamin Steinitz gave an essential feature, an eighteenth-century oak parquet floor (the original floor had been sold). Steinitz also advised on the project and managed aspects of the restoration program in Paris.

Finally, again based on more recent research by Pons, and further back to that of the decorative-arts historian Pierre Verlet, a new program of furniture—including armchairs, *canapé*, side chairs, and consoles—was conceived to reflect more accurately the eighteenth-century furnishing of a *salon de compagnie* (reception room). The furniture needed to interact more closely with the architecture, to tell the social history of how such *salons de compagnie* functioned in the aristocratic *hôtel* before the Revolution.

LIGHTING

Lighting is an essential aspect of period rooms. Previously, and in line with the standard principle of museum renovation of the early 1990s, spotlights and tracks were set into the ceiling, and the historic fixtures were stripped of their candles.[6] To recapture the domestic character of this space, it seemed important to base the new lighting on historic light fixtures wherever possible, with discreet additions. Research led us to utilize objects already in the collection, including wall lights, a chandelier, and a grand pair of torchères. With our directions to illuminate the room based on candlelight in the historic fixtures, the San Francisco–based lighting company Auerbach Glasow French devised a plan. Having introduced an atmospheric lighting scheme in the Wrightsman rooms of the Metropolitan Museum in the early 2000s, the company had experience in dealing with the challenges of lighting period rooms. With electric candles placed in all the fixtures, lighting concealed in the chandelier and the stanchions, and "glow" lights secreted in the wall lights and torchères (a technique suggested by Steinitz), the overall impression is of a room lit by candlelight, while not appearing too dim for modern eyes used to the brilliance of electric light.

CONSERVATION

Conservation of the paneling was an essential precondition to the new installation. Some of the carving had been damaged, and the gilding had suffered successive campaigns of restoration, some worse than others. Starting from the premise that new gilding can look harsh and lack character, we decided—on the advice of Steinitz and the knowledge of our museum gilder, Natasa Morovic—to clean and repair the existing gilding wherever possible. Steinitz and Morovic suspected that the gilding was largely done in the nineteenth century (which turned out to be the case), but layers occasionally appeared underneath, which included the earliest eighteenth-century layer.

The original carving was of the highest quality, with crisp and lively details in trophies surmounting the mirrors and laurel pendants flanking the door cases. However, in re-creating parts of missing sections, much thought was needed to determine the intentions of the creators.

Master carver Adam Thorpe took on the complex task of painstakingly crafting such details as the flowers, leaves, and ribbons of the trophies above the mirrors (fig. 5), recarving sections to match, sometimes more than once, to get the perspective exactly right.

The paint color of the paneling was another major question: samples revealed many campaigns of redecoration, more than twenty in the central panel of one of the doors. Under layers of green, cream, and dark gray appeared a very pale gray, a color that was subsequently confirmed by the inventory of the Salon taken in 1790 after the death of the duchess. (For more on the original color, see the inventory and Lesley Bone's essay in this volume.) The color was also found in the recent restoration of a salon of this era in the Hôtel Saint-Florentin/de Talleyrand, in Paris.[7]

The plaster overdoors, which depict the Nymphs dancing and sacrificing to Love, were painted dark gray (probably for the first Legion installation) and were likely originally supplied by the sculptor Pierre Fixon (active 1748–1788), who specialized in making such decorations (see a similar overdoor in fig. 1).[8] Black-and-white photographs of the overdoors from 1905 indicate a very different color—white, or at least a very light color. When the modern paint was removed, a

FIG. 5. Detail of the carved giltwood trophy above one of the Salon Doré's four mirrors. This wreath, bound by a meandering ribbon with a flaming torch and a quiver of arrows, forms an emblem of Love—and Venus. This photograph shows the carving restored by Adam Thorpe and the new gilding before it was harmonized with the old gilding.

beige similar to that of limestone (which was the stone used in Parisian masonry) was revealed in the original layer (see fig. 63), which has now been conserved and reinstated.

The whole conservation was overseen by the Museums' head objects conservator, Lesley Bone, who initiated tests on several aspects, notably the paint, supervised the complex dismantling of the many pieces of paneling, and organized a program for their conservation, which is further described in her essay in this volume.

FURNITURE

The most crucial aspect beyond the paneling, the lighting, and the new architectural features was the furnishing of the room. In the conventional French period room in American museums, fine examples of *ébénisterie* (cabinetwork), luxurious commodes, delicate tables, and writing desks dominate (see fig. 1), but before the Revolution these *salons de compagnie* were, in fact, furnished principally with chairs. Rows of giltwood chairs and sofas were arranged to receive guests in the salons of the *hôtels particuliers*. This mode of furnishing, which has been largely lost or forgotten until recently, had yet to be properly re-created in an American museum presentation, so the Salon restoration was the opportunity to do so.

The chairs consisted of two ranks, armchairs and side chairs. Armchairs were arranged around the walls in concert with the architecture of the paneling (see fig. 6). This so-called *meuble*, *mobilier d'architecture*, *mobilier meublant*, or even *mobilier dormant* was rarely, if ever, moved or used. Side chairs (known variously as *chaises* or *sièges courants*, *volants*, or *d'usage*) were designated for guests to sit on, and were often arranged in a conversational U or circle in the middle of the room. The aim was not lounging comfort but a measured formality to reflect the elevated status of the owners and the etiquette of gatherings (see figs. 21 and 22). In rarely allowing anyone to use the armchairs set against the walls, the eighteenth-century aristocrats of Paris reflected the social hierarchy that Louis XIV had imposed on his court at Versailles, where only certain people could sit in the presence of the king.

Aside from this profusion of seats, the only other pieces of permanent furniture were giltwood console tables, which were set between the windows and opposite the chimneypiece, and were designed to complement the paneling. Highly finished cabinets, including commodes, were usually reserved for the more private living spaces, such as the bedroom or dressing room. For more informal occasions when the family was at home—as depicted in the print *L'assemblé au salon* (see fig. 23)—small tables for writing and sewing, as well as card tables and trictrac tables for gaming, could be brought into the room.

Inspired by those depicted in one salon designed for the duchesse de Mazarin, the armchairs deemed most appropriate for our Salon in terms of style, size, and quality are part of a set of six Louis XVI armchairs (*fauteuils à la reine*, or straight-backed armchairs, to set against the wall) from a suite made for Guillaume Périer, vicomte de Grèzes (1720–1790), for his apartments at the Hôtel de Toulouse, Paris. Périer was a *fermier-général* who also ran the estates for one of the richest men in France at that time, the duc de Penthièvre. The chairs, in the Neoclassical style, with square, flat backs, made with the high quality expected of a chair maker such as Georges Jacob

FIG. 6. François-Joseph Bélanger (French, 1744–1818), elevation of a wall in the salon of the duchesse de Mazarin, drawn ca. 1780. Pen, ink, and watercolor on paper, 16 5/16 × 20 7/8 in. (41.5 × 53 cm). Victoria and Albert Museum, London. This drawing shows how seat furniture was arranged along the walls in the grand Parisian aristocratic salon.

(see cat. no. 6), were commensurate with the paneling. Furthermore, they are of the correct height for the room's chair rail so that they integrate successfully with the paneling. Based on other inventories (before the discovery of the 1790 inventory of the Hôtel de La Trémoille), such as that of the Hôtel d'Orsay in the Corcoran Gallery of Art in Washington, DC, the number of armchairs determined to be appropriate was eight.[9] Thus only two additional armchairs had to be made by joiners in Paris, as well as a *canapé*, which had also been described in the inventories.

For the *chaises courantes*, the collection already included a set of four *chaises en cabriolet* (side chairs with slightly rounded backs), dated around 1780, with a royal provenance of the Château de Saint-Leu, which in the 1780s belonged to the duc de Penthièvre's daughter, the duchesse d'Orléans (Marie-Adélaide de Bourbon-Penthièvre, 1753–1821; see cat. no. 8). By chance, another six side chairs with the same horseshoe-shaped backs (but not from the same set), stamped by Jacob, were on the market in Paris and were purchased to make a set of ten (see cat. no. 7). Based on Xavier Bonnet's research in the archives, such salons contained as many as twelve or fifteen side chairs, but eventually the inventory of 1790 confirmed that the Salon held ten *sièges courants*. Even more exciting for accuracy, the chairs from Saint-Leu had the remains of a highly appropriate inscription on their labels: *Chaise Courante du Salon*. All that needed to be added was a pair of *bergères*, to fulfill their presence in the inventory and to reflect their significance in the social history of the Parisian salon during these years (see Alexandre Pradère's essay in this volume). A pair of *bergères* that suited this task (see cat. no. 9), similar in design to that of the armchairs, was identified in the collection and brought the total number of seats to an impressive twenty-one, only four fewer than described in the inventory of 1790.

With respect to the consoles, the originals were described in contemporary documents as being supplied by the *menuisier* Sené.[10] Another contemporary account detailed the design's elaborate carving in the frieze, which had a floral wreath set above a sunburst at the center and scrolled bracket supports hung with garlands and set with a vase underneath.[11] The consoles also had white marble slabs to match the marble of the chimneypiece.[12] After an extensive search, one giltwood console on the Paris market was identified that was of suitable Neoclassical *goût grec* style (the earliest, muscular expression of the Neoclassical style in 1760s and 1770s France) Derived from one of Richard de Lalonde's drawings (fig. 7), it had the appropriate proportions and, most important, the dimensions to work with the paneling. In general terms, it matched the design of the Salon's consoles noted in the contemporary document. To complete the essential architectural interplay between the paneling and the consoles, the second console needed to be wider and had to be fabricated. The construction of the console, as well as that of the armchairs and sofa, introduces questions about authenticity of works in this project. However, since the paneling is the principal player in this story, many elements in the room—from the ceiling to the windows, the textiles, and some of the furniture and gilt bronzes—are necessarily modern copies in order to complete the overall picture of the Salon as an architectural entity (see the checklist in this volume).

FIG. 7. After Richard de Lalonde (French, active 1780–1790), *Oeuvres diverses de Lalonde décorateur et dessinateur; Ve Cahier E. Table et consoles avec leurs plans* (*Various Works of Lalonde, Decorator and Designer; Fifth Book, E. Table and Consoles with Their Plans*), ca. 1775–1789. Etching, 13 9/16 × 8 9/16 in. (34.5 × 21.8 cm). Victoria and Albert Museum, London.

UPHOLSTERY AND TEXTILES

Choosing the most appropriate pattern and color of silk for the upholstery and curtains proved to be a surprisingly difficult task. The expert in historic upholstery Xavier Bonnet, who had worked on the restoration of the Swan suite in the Museum of Fine Arts, Boston, and several chairs for the Musée des Arts Décoratifs, Paris, advised on the textiles and upholstery for our Salon. With so many available choices of silk lampas (a luxury silk fabric similar to brocade, with wefts of a taffeta background and a design on top), this part of the refurbishment initially seemed easy, but only after protracted research was a pattern based on a document of the 1780s identified—one that suited the design and scale of the Salon. The choice of color was even more exacting. Based on inventories, crimson had been our first choice, but when the 1790 inventory of the Salon was found (see pp. 97–99 in this volume), it described the color scheme of the silk as blue and white. We therefore elected to use documentary examples in the Musée Historique des Tissus in Lyon as the model for the design and the color (see figs. 43, 44).

The design of the upholstery was gently guided by Bonnet, who favored simpler, rounded forms for the chairs rather than the elaborate *piqure à l'anglaise* (English stitching, with boxed edges) often found on recent interpretations of historic upholstery. He also chose to employ different motifs on the backs of the chairs so as to waste as little silk as possible—a return to eighteenth-century practice advocated by Bonnet and found up to now only on the upholstery of Boston's Swan suite.[13] The design of the curtains was derived from a drawing in the Cooper-Hewitt, National

Design Museum (fig. 47), which had already served as a model for curtains in the Metropolitan Museum.[14] Few, if any, surviving examples of French eighteenth-century window curtains were suitable in terms of both the date and the style. Along with the fabric, the design shows how the two curtains were positioned under a draped and fringed valence and how they were caught up with ties to lift their tails from the floor.

MIRRORS

Mirrors were considered the most expensive and, in some ways, the most important features of a salon. They provide seemingly infinite reflections when placed opposite each other and enhance the illumination of a room—an important consideration when one considers the dim light of candles, which was augmented only by the use of gilding and light paint colors. Plate-glass mirrors made in the eighteenth century were backed with mercury, which over time gives a deep gray reflection that is sometimes flecked with attractive sparkles. Although given pride of place in the inventories, the mirrors were often not assigned values because they were assumed to be permanent fixtures of the house (see "History of the Salon" in this volume). However, as they were worth very high sums, many mirrors were removed and sold during the Revolution, and it is likely that this happened to at least one of the mirrors in the Salon of the Hôtel de La Trémoille.

Because so few of these essential features are present in French period rooms in the United States, composing a complete set of mercury mirror plates for this project seemed highly desirable. Three of the mirrors in the Legion's original gift are mercury backed. The replacement mirror for the one removed for the Kahn mansion installation in 1918, when a doorway was inserted, was of modern industrial manufacture (with an even reflection and bland color) and was out of balance with the others. Dealer Pierre-Olivier Chanel gave the museum a mercury-style mirror, which has restored a sense of harmony in this important area.

DISCOVERY OF AN INVENTORY

Years into the planning for the Salon and with the project well under way, Bonnet discovered an inventory of the Salon in the Archives Nationales, Paris, taken after the death of the duchesse de La Trémoille in July 1790.[15] Reassuringly, it confirmed much of what we had determined, but it also posed several important and complicated questions. In broad terms, the furnishings were as we had anticipated: four mirrors, two console tables, armchairs arranged around the walls, *sièges courants* for use in the middle of the room, curtains, three-branched wall lights, one twelve-light chandelier, one clock, and even a garniture of three blue vases.

However, the inventory cited a surprisingly large number of seats, fifty-one in total, which, compared to other salons of the era, seemed far too numerous.[16] Considering the size of the room, about twenty-six feet square, this description added up to more chairs than were practically useful; one would have had to climb over them to get from one side of the room to the other. The answer to the question of this excessive number, detailed in "History of the Salon," was that an extra set of chairs was stored in the Salon at the time the inventory was taken. By 1790 the duke and duchess had emigrated on the pretext that the duchess, "for her health," needed to go to Nice (then in Savoy rather than France), where she died (thus necessitating the inventory). The house had been closed up and the furniture was under dust covers when the appraiser came to record the objects present at that moment.

The inventory also described an unexpected color scheme for the room. Previously we had planned to use crimson upholstery, based on other inventory descriptions of the time and the convention that the color represented the status of aristocracy. But when the Salon inventory stated that the formal furnishing armchairs, sofa, and curtains were covered in a *damas bleu et blanc* (blue and white damask), we knew we needed to follow that path instead. Furthermore, the paneling was described as *gris rechampis en or* (gray highlighted with gold). This color had already been discovered in the paint samples, but it raised the question of how to follow this newly discovered color scheme successfully. Would it work with worn gilding—or would it look too cold? The blue and white textile was difficult to re-create, as so few examples of upholstery silk from that era survive, and even fewer are blue. Determining the correct blue to work with the pattern we had already chosen was also a challenge. The blue, like the pattern, was eventually drawn from a silk document in the Musée Historique des Tissus in Lyon and from drawings, such as that of the salon of the Hôtel de Salm (see fig. 40).[17]

CONCLUSION

The aim of this project was to conserve the paneling and to reinstall it in the manner closest to its origins in eighteenth-century Paris. It was also to reconfigure the room as an architectural entity by reinstating the parquet floor, the windows, two of the sets of doors, and other furnishings according to eighteenth-century principles. Because of the high quality of its design and craftsmanship, the *boiserie* became the focus of this project. Although the furniture is not original to the room and new architectural elements have been added, the Legion's Salon is now the only Parisian salon in an American museum that contains its full complement of armchairs and sofa as the *mobilier meublant* arranged around the walls and engaged with the paneling, with a second set of *chaises courantes* situated in the center of the room. Indeed, it may be the only aristocratic salon from a Parisian *hôtel* displayed in this manner anywhere.

Unlike the traditional French period room, the Salon includes no carpets or luxury pieces of *ébénisterie*—only giltwood consoles and chairs. Whenever appropriate, we installed furniture and decorative arts from the existing museum collections, such as the grand garniture of Sèvres vases (dating from the 1760s) and the torchères with figures by Jean-François Lorta (of about 1780). The lately discovered 1790 inventory of the Salon presented new demands for interpretation, but it also informed important aspects of this project, such as the color of the walls and upholstery as well as the number of seats. Within the confines of modern research and modern installation requirements, and with a modern audience in mind, this interpretation of the *salon de compagnie* is much closer to an eighteenth-century Parisian interior than previous period rooms. Although it is an interpretation of our own time, we want this Salon from the Hôtel de La Trémoille to stand as an example of how the period room can remain authentic and engaging in the museum of the twenty-first century.

NOTES

1 The Louis XV Room from Rouen, ca. 1750, was the only room brought to the Legion of Honor. All of the other period rooms were dispersed.
2 Lecture to the European Decorative Arts Council of the Fine Arts Museums, April 13, 2011. The other significant period rooms include the Salon Doré in the Corcoran Gallery of Art, Washington, DC, and the Grand Salon from the Hôtel de Tessé and the Crillon cabinet in the Metropolitan Museum of Art, New York.
3 *Le faubourg Saint-Germain: La rue Saint-Dominique: Hôtels et amateurs* (Paris, 1984), 72.
4 Archives Nationales, Paris. The author is grateful to Nicolas Personne for finding the plans at the archives and obtaining photographs.
5 Bruno Pons, *French Period Rooms, 1650–1800: Rebuilt in England, France, and the Americas* (Dijon, 1995). This tended to be less true by the 1780s, when salons in newly built houses, such as the Hôtel Grimod de La Reynière, were rectangular. Although the paneling from our Salon dates to 1781, the original footprint for the room was built in 1707, thus utilizing the square dimensions.
6 This change was in accordance with the view that candles were never left in chandeliers or wall lights in the eighteenth century. However, from the evidence of prints such as *L'assemblé au salon* (fig. 23), candles have now been furnished in all the fixtures.
7 Fabrice Ouziel, the historical architect for this project, was very helpful about the gray that he found there.
8 Pons, *French Period Rooms*, 293–294.
9 "Item a three-seat sofa in carved gilded wood in different colors of gold and eight matching armchairs all upholstered with crimson and flowered Gobelins tapestry"; Dare Myers Hartwell and Bruno Pons, *The Salon Doré* (Washington, DC, 1998), 30.
10 *Le faubourg Saint-Germain*.
11 Archives Nationales, Paris, T//1051/55, *Papiers La Trémoille*.
12 *Le faubourg Saint-Germain*, 72.
13 Museum of Fine Arts, Boston. Part of a suite of bedroom furniture, including a *bergère*, 36.640; bed, 21.1265; kneeling chair, 53.2092; fire screen, 27.533; two armchairs, 50.2342 and 53.2851; and four side chairs, 27.524, 27.525, 47.244, and 53.2850; probably acquired by James Swan of Boston, 1794–1796.
14 The author is grateful to Daniëlle Kisluk-Grosheide for her advice about curtains as well as her thoughts about the many questions surrounding the recent reinstallation of the Hôtel de Tessé room in the Wrightsman galleries, a room that bears many similarities to the Salon of the Hôtel de La Trémoille.
15 Archives Nationales, Paris, MC/ET/LVII/597 (see pp. 97–99 in this volume).
16 There were twenty-one to twenty-seven seats in the salon of the Hôtel d'Orsay, fourteen to twenty-eight in the salon of the Hôtel d'Uzès, and thirty-one in Samuel Bernard's salon in 1753; Pons, *French Period Rooms*, 147, 328.
17 See Alexandre Gady, *Les hôtels particuliers de Paris du Moyen Âge à la Belle Époque* (Paris, 2008).

HISTORY OF THE SALON

Martin Chapman

In his 2007 book, *Moving Rooms*, the architectural historian John Harris argues that one of the prevailing characteristics of historic paneling is that it moves—and continues to move. That statement is certainly true of the *boiserie* of the Salon Doré, which has been installed no fewer than eight times during its 230 or so years of existence, and this essay traces the paneling backwards, from this new installation to its original birthplace in Paris.

The paneling arrived at the Legion of Honor in 1959 as a gift from the museum trustee Richard Rheem, whose family manufactured hot-water heaters in the Bay Area. Rheem had acquired the paneling from the New York art dealers Duveen Brothers in 1955, when he installed it as the ballroom in his mansion, La Dolphine, in Hillsborough, south of San Francisco. The *boiserie* came from Duveen with a very grand yet spurious provenance: supposedly it had originated at the Hôtel de Crillon in the place de la Concorde, Paris, designed by the architect Ange-Jacques Gabriel (1698–1782).

The Salon was the first period room installed in the Legion of Honor (although an English room also was considered at the same time but was not acquired).[1] From 1960, the paneling was installed in the Legion under the guidance of Winfield Scott Wellington (1897–1979), who discovered its true provenance in the Hôtel d'Humières, Paris, and who mounted it at the Legion based on that location.[2] Wellington, an architect and professor of design at the University of California, Berkeley, cleverly reconfigured the paneling to match the dimensions of the original Salon in the Hôtel d'Humières.

"The Duke," as Wellington was known, used early photographs of the Salon to re-create the plaster frieze and cornice. He assembled the paneling as a typical period room, with the architectural components traditional for such a room—a ceiling with a gilded rosette, windows, and a parquet

FIG. 8 (*above*). The first installation of the Salon Doré at the Legion of Honor opened in 1962. It included a parquet floor, plain ceiling with a gilded rosette, windows, and some French furniture from the museum's collection.

FIG. 9 (*right*). Winfield Scott Wellington, *Preliminary Study #2 of Window Wall—Louis 16th Room, California Palace of the Legion of Honor— San Francisco*, April 16, 1960. Pencil on drafting paper, 12 × 18½ in. (30.5 × 47 cm). Environmental Design Archives, University of California, Berkeley.

floor, all of which were omitted in the Legion's later installation; and he furnished it with some of the finest French furniture in the museum's collections (see fig. 8). Although the files on this installation have not been found, Wellington's early sketches of the paneling's installation survive in archives at the university (fig. 9) and show that he understood the principles of eighteenth-century French architecture—even though, under his guidance, the Salon was eventually built with windows that were much wider than the originals and thus looked stretched in proportion. The *boiserie* has been reinstalled in the Legion twice since then, including the present display.

Why the incorrect Crillon provenance was promoted to Rheem is not revealed in the Duveen Records.[3] What is clear, however, is that in 1955 Duveen Brothers sold Rheem three rooms for La Dolphine (fig. 10): the "Crillon Room" (the Salon) for a ballroom; Louis XV paneling for the library; and Louis XV paneling from a house on rue de Richelieu for a dining room.[4] The Parisian decorating firm Decour then installed them at La Dolphine.[5] Duveen Brothers sent a maquette, or model, of the Crillon Room to San Francisco in 1954, probably to convince Rheem to buy it.[6] The model, which was returned to New York and then sent back to San Francisco a few years

FIG. 10. La Dolphine, Hillsborough, California, estate of Mr. and Mrs. Richard Rheem, ca. 1960. Photograph by Slim Aarons.

FIG. 11 (*above*). Maquette provided by Duveen Brothers at the time of the Rheems' purchase of the Salon Doré interior. Full flattened three-dimensional model, French, ca. 1950. Wood with hand-colored paper on card, 8¾ × 21 × 13 in. (22.2 × 53.3 × 33 cm).

FIG. 12 (*right*). The Salon Doré installed at Duveen Brothers' showrooms, New York, 1946–1947.

later, when Rheem gave the room to the Legion, miraculously survives in the Museums' collection (fig. 11).[7] It shows the elongated form of the Salon when the decorating firm Alavoine first set it up at the Duveen Brothers premises at 720 Fifth Avenue in about 1934.[8] Edward Fowles justified the acquisition of the room for Duveen Brothers as an important backdrop to their French furniture from the Hillingdon collection.[9] He recalled in a letter to Dr. James Rorimer, director of the Metropolitan Museum of Art, New York, that the late proprietor of the firm, Lord Duveen (1869–1939), wanted to use the *boiserie* as a background because he felt that "the finest French furniture of that collection [the Wallace Collection, London] displayed in normal museum surroundings could not be appreciated at its real artistic value, and had none of the *éclat*."[10] As well as the maquette, photographs from this Duveen installation show that the paneling was reconfigured to just under forty feet long and that showcases were inserted into the end walls.[11] This installation also served as the background for a charity exhibition of French furniture held at Duveen Brothers in 1946 and 1947 (see figs. 12, 69).

For the generation prior to Duveen Brothers' acquisition of the paneling, the room had served as the "French salon" at the core of banker Otto Kahn's great Italian Renaissance–style mansion at 1 East 91st Street in New York, overlooking Fifth Avenue. Touted as one of the largest private mansions ever built in that city, the eighty-room Otto Kahn mansion was designed by the architect J. Armstrong Stenhouse after the papal chancellery in Rome. Stenhouse placed the French salon nearly opposite the mansion's Adam ballroom and next to the gothic art gallery, demonstrating that the concept of period rooms was already flourishing in the private mansions of the Gilded Age long before it became standard in American museums (see fig. 13). A photograph of the French salon in the Kahn mansion reveals that it was set up with a nearly square configuration but with one of the mirrors replaced by an additional doorway, making five sets of doors into the room that had originally only had four (and therefore there were three mirrors instead of the initial four) (fig. 14).[12] Where Kahn himself acquired the paneling is as yet unknown. Given the time period, the most likely source would have been the Paris paneling dealer Carlhian (active 1867–1975). Carlhian was, indeed, asked to do work on the Kahn residence, such as the music room in 1915 and 1916, and on installing the Salon, but there is no evidence in the surviving archives that the firm sold the room to Kahn.[13] The likely source is Alavoine, a French decorator based in New York, which is mentioned in the Carlhian Records as storing the paneling and may well have sold the *boiserie* to Kahn.

The Hôtel d'Humières, on rue de Lille, was a *cause célèbre* when it was demolished in 1905.[14] Its destruction was regarded as one of the greatest architectural losses of the day, and the Société d'histoire et d'archéologie du VIIe arrondissement (the historical society for the seventh district in Paris, founded in 1903) archived an extensive series of photographs of the mansion taken before its demolition. Although one corner of its courtyard already had been truncated by the extension of the boulevard Saint-Germain in 1873, this grand private house was not so much a victim of Haussmann's urban plans as it was a casualty

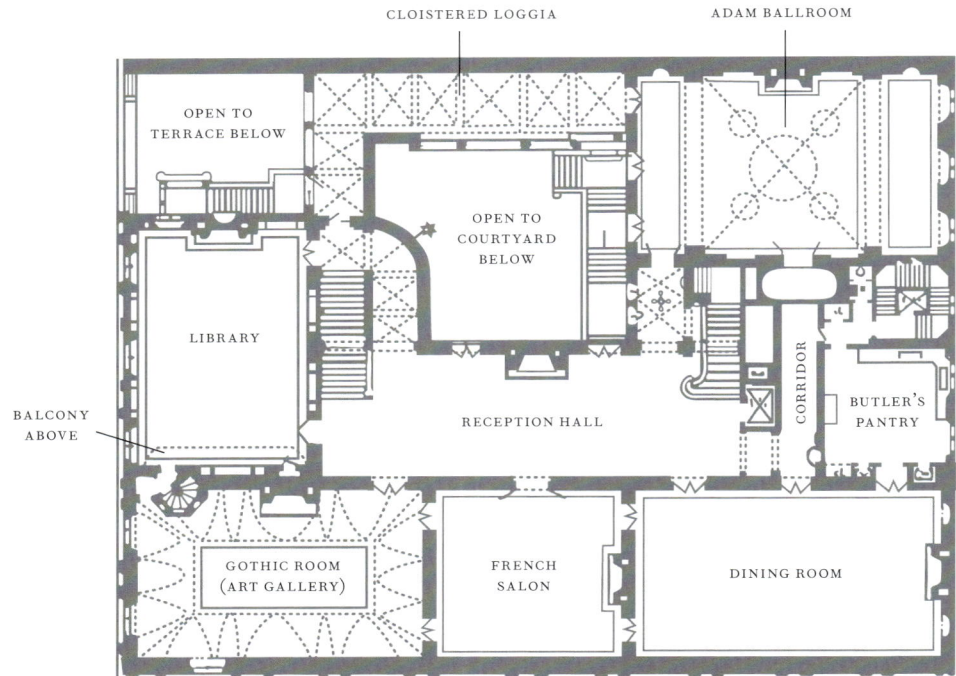

FIG. 13 (*left*). Plan of the second floor of the Otto Kahn mansion, New York, drawing after Richard Marchand.

FIG. 14 (*below*). Otto Kahn mansion, New York, with the Salon Doré installed, before 1934.

of Paris's booming prosperity at the turn of the twentieth century.¹⁵ The house and its grounds gave way to several apartment buildings constructed to house the burgeoning middle classes of the Belle Époque.

The *boiserie* had been installed in the *hôtel*'s ground-floor salon, overlooking the garden, and photographs taken in the year of its destruction reveal the room's appearance at that time (figs. 4, 15). It was still furnished in the luxurious style of the Second Empire, with a thick Savonnerie-style carpet, overstuffed and tufted seat furniture arranged in conversational groups, elaborate wall sconces with several branches each, and large mounted vases on stands.¹⁶ The eighteenth-century plan of the Hôtel d'Humières, published

FIG. 15. Detail of the fireplace wall from the Salon Doré installation at the Hôtel d'Humières, ca. 1905. Société d'histoire et d'archéologie du VIIe arrondissement de Paris.

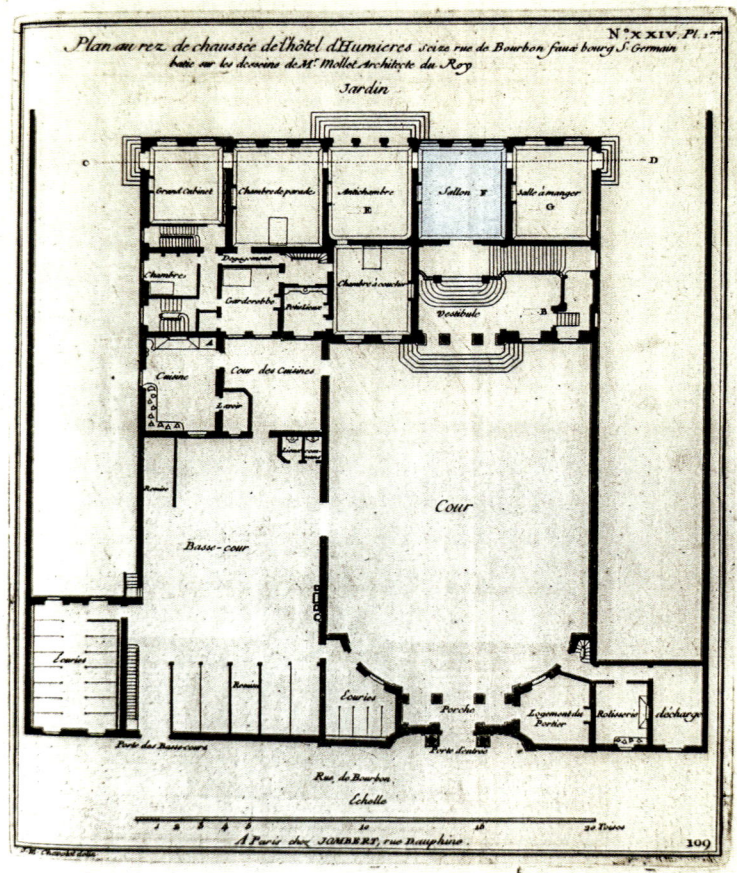

FIG. 16. Jacques-François Blondel (French, 1705–1774), floor plan of the Hôtel d'Humières, from *L'Architecture françoise* (Paris, 1752–1756). The *boiserie* was installed on the ground floor, here identified as "Sallon F."

in Jacques-François Blondel's *L'Architecture françoise* (fig. 16), reveals that the Salon was approximately thirty-one feet square, the dimensions that Wellington used for his Legion reinstallation in 1960–1962. It also shows that the room contained three windows rather than two, which indicates that there were questions about the proportions of the room that would be answered only by new research; thus the stretched proportions of the two windows in Wellington's installation at the Legion. This eventually was resolved by the surprising discovery of an earlier provenance for the Salon.

The architectural historian Bruno Pons, who specialized in the history of the paneling of the Parisian *hôtel*, published documentation of this *boiserie* several times over the years. After first citing it in his catalogue of the exhibition on rue de Lille, in 1983, he followed this up with accounts that increasingly introduced doubts that the paneling had originated in the Hôtel d'Humières.[17] Finally, in a 1996 catalogue of paneling from Waddesdon Manor, England, he definitively established that it had an earlier provenance: the vanished Hôtel de La Trémoille (see fig. 17).[18] Most of the paneling from the Hôtel d'Humières had been placed in the East and West Galleries at Waddesdon in the 1870s, long before the *hôtel* itself was demolished. Thus, Pons argued, our *boiserie* must have been the Louis XVI paneling that was described as being moved into the Hôtel d'Humières by the marquise de Croix. She had been displaced from the Hôtel de La Trémoille in 1877 when that *hôtel* on rue Saint-Dominique was demolished due to Haussmann's extending the boulevard Saint-Germain through the neighborhood in 1877.[19] The former Hôtel de La Trémoille was, therefore, the true origin of this paneling, not the Hôtel d'Humières, where it was installed much later, between 1879 and 1905.

This new provenance revealed an entirely fresh history for the paneling and allows us to look still deeper into its origins. According to Pons's research, the *boiserie* was installed in the Hôtel de La Trémoille in 1781 at the time of the marriage of the La Trémoilles' eldest son, Charles Bretagne

FIG. 17. Jean-Michel Chevotet (French, 1698–1772), facade of the *galerie*, facing the gardens, of the Hôtel Bethune (later the Hôtel de Châtillon and the Hôtel de La Trémoille). Drawing for the etching in Jacques-François Blondel, *L'Architecture françoise* (Paris, 1752–1756). École nationale supérieure des Beaux-Arts, Paris. The *boiserie* was installed in the Salon behind the two rightmost windows below the central pediment. The drawing has been reversed for the purposes of engraving.

Marie, prince de Tarente (1764–1839), to Louise-Emmanuelle de Châtillon (1763–1814). It was incorporated into the garden wing of an existing house, built between 1705 and 1707 and designed by the architect Pierre Cailleteau, known as Lassurance (1655–1724), originally called the Hôtel de Neuchâtel and later renamed for its subsequent owners, as the Hôtel de Béthune and then the Hôtel de Châtillon. The prince de Tarente's marriage was dynastic, and Louise-Emmanuelle, the younger daughter of the extremely wealthy duc de Châtillon, inherited the house (then the Hôtel de Châtillon) from her father. The wedding of 1781 was a grand affair: the princesse de Rohan lent a four-poster bed from the Hôtel de Soubise for the event, the newly named Hôtel de La Trémoille was illuminated with lamps, and fireworks were set off. The family made lavish expenditure on the new princess's requisite emblems of status, such as two toilet services supplied by the dealers Daguerre and Le Roy and lace and other luxuries for her trousseau. However, it was not a happy marriage—as is revealed in the memoirs of both parties.[20] The prince was described as "dissipated" by his biographer Winifred Stephens Whale, and his journals indicate that he thought his wife was ugly and that he had married her only for her money.[21] The princess later became one of Marie-Antoinette's most devoted ladies-in-waiting. After she was imprisoned during the Revolution, the princess escaped and moved to London, where she wrote her memoirs. There she lived separately from her husband, who managed to fall out with the Prince Regent by refusing the military regiment offered to him.[22] Finally she departed for the court at Saint Petersburg, where she

FIG. 18. Unknown artist, *Jean Bretagne, Duc de La Trémoille, Marie de Salm, Duchesse de La Trémoille, and Their Sons*, illustration in Winifred Stephens Whale, *The La Trémoille Family* (Boston and New York: Houghton Mifflin Company, 1914).

died. The prince lived on to have two more marriages and additional children.

The family accounts indicate that the duc and duchesse de La Trémoille paid rent to their daughter-in-law.[23] The duc and duchesse de La Trémoille lived in apartments on the same floor (rather than one above the other, on separate floors, as was usual in Paris; see Alexandre Pradère's essay in this volume) in the main grand apartments, overlooking the garden, in a series of splendid rooms that flanked the Salon, where the new *boiserie* was installed. This part of the house was arranged as an *appartement de société*, furnished according to the La Trémoilles' rank as premier dukes and foreign princes in France. The house's *salle du dais* (a canopy room denoting the status of the duke or prince) was the main antechamber preceding the Salon, and the house had formal bedchambers and related apartments for the duke and duchess. In one of his essays in this volume, Xavier Bonnet describes in detail the Hôtel de La Trémoille's furnishing.

The La Trémoilles were an ancient family, with vast estates in western France centered on Thouars and another estate at Attichy, near Compiègne, where the duke placed a great fountain of Neptune in the gardens.[24] Closely associated with the history of France for more than five centuries, the La Trémoille dukes had a long tradition of serving in the army. In the 1780s, the family bore two princely titles, Tarente and Talmond; as premier dukes of France, they were ranked just below the royal family in the French hierarchy. They even had a claim to the throne of Naples through their sixteenth-century ancestor Anne de Laval (1505–1554).

Jean-Bretagne-Charles de La Trémoille (1737–1792) was a soldier who fought in the Seven Years' War. In 1763, he married his second wife, Marie-Maximilienne, princess of Salm-Kyrburg (a principality in the German Rhineland), with whom he had four sons (see fig. 18). During the Revolution, he served with the royalist armies in Savoy, where he died, and two of his sons—the prince de Talmond and the abbé de La Trémoille—were executed during the Reign of Terror in 1794. The duchess was the sister of Prince Frederick III of Salm-Kyrburg, who built the famous Hôtel de Salm between 1782 and 1788 on rue de Lille, overlooking the banks of the Seine (see fig. 19). Much admired by Thomas Jefferson, it was regarded as one of the modern architectural wonders of Paris. It is remarkable that the Salon from the Hôtel de La Trémoille is now situated within the Legion of Honor—a building based on the Hôtel de Salm—and that these two Neoclassical structures, so closely linked by family ties, are united in San Francisco.

Family archives (now in the Archives Nationales, Paris) describe the Salon of the La

FIG. 19. Unknown artist (French, eighteenth century), *The Construction of the Hôtel de Salm, Paris, in 1786*, ca. 1786. Oil on canvas, 22¼ × 39¾ in. (56.5 × 101 cm). Musée de la Ville de Paris, Musée Carnavalet, Paris.

Trémoilles as having two console tables designed by the architect Pierre-Auguste Delapoize,[25] made by Séné, sculpted by Royer, and gilded by Royer *fils* for the room's installation in 1781.[26] The documentation also mentions that a stove was installed for the gilders' use, but no accounts in the archives detail the actual making of the Salon. However, as the Archives Nationales documents show, the whole *appartement de société* of the duc and duchesse de La Trémoille was completely refurbished in these years (see Xavier Bonnet's essays in this volume), so therefore it is certain that the paneling for the Salon was created at this time.

Bonnet recently rediscovered the 1790 inventory of the Salon, which reveals much about how the room was furnished at that date. The four mirrors, considered some of the costliest assets of the house, are described in detail and their dimensions cited (which helped us to verify the Salon's provenance in the house). The inventory notes that the mirrors were set into gray-painted, gilded paneling, but they were not assigned a value, as they were expected to remain part of the fixtures and fittings of the house.[27] Such was commonly the case when inventories were taken after a death, but during the Revolution, mirrors and paneling were no longer revered as fixtures and often were sold off. The Hôtel de La Trémoille was seized in 1794 and its furniture sold.[28] Thereafter, the Ministry of War used it as offices. By the time of the fall of Napoleon, the house was restituted to the former owners; but rather than returning to the La Trémoilles, it went to the duchesse d'Uzès, sister of Louise-Emmanuelle, the princesse de Tarente, who had died in Saint Petersburg in 1814. In 1815, the outgoing occupant, General Marescot, *inspecteur général du génie*, had an inventory made of the Salon. It notes that the structure of the Salon had survived remarkably intact, but that the room had lost one of its mirrors.[29]

The 1790 inventory discloses important aspects of the Salon that were not previously known, such as the paneling's color scheme of gray and the blue and white silk used for the upholstery and curtains. The room's giltwood consoles with white marble tops appear in greater detail in a *mémoire* (account), dated in the 1780s, by the gilder Royer, who charged 816 *livres* for the two (although they were valued at only 200 *livres* in the 1790 inventory).[30]

To the two pairs of gilt-bronze wall lights was added a third pair because the 1790 appraiser viewed these as part of the fireplace furniture, which was extensive and included firedogs (andirons) with gilt-bronze vases, bellows, a polished steel fireguard of six panels, and two small horsehair brooms. The chimneypiece shelf was decorated with a garniture of three large blue and white porcelain vases, two small rock-crystal girandoles (candelabra) mounted in gilt bronze with feet painted to resemble lacquer, and two jasper vases—a rather motley crew of objects that reveals just how crowded such chimneypieces could be. The gilt-bronze clock by Ledunois, inventoried for 600 *livres*, is not a surprise; neither is the twelve-light chandelier of white rock crystal, or the glass case fitted over two vases of artificial flowers (possibly made of wax, as was an example in the inventory of the salon of the Hôtel d'Orsay) in their porcelain bowls.[31]

A puzzling item in the 1790 inventory is the composition and color of the Salon's seat furniture. Fifty-one seats were inventoried, which seems excessive for a room of its size (about twenty-six feet

FIG. 20. Louis Nicolas van Blarenberghe (French, 1716–1794) and Henri Joseph van Blarenberghe (French, 1741–1826), snuffbox depicting the duc de Choiseul, chief minister to Louis XV, in the salon of his *hôtel* on the rue de Richelieu, Paris. Image: 3¾ × 5 in. (9.6 × 12.7 cm). Jay Robert Nash Collection. This view depicts the practice of arranging armchairs along the walls. It is also evident that some chairs with different upholstery have strayed from another room.

square). Even more perturbing is that the inventory lists two suites of color schemes, one of blue and white silk that made up the *mobilier d'architecture* and a second set of twenty-two chairs covered in crimson Utrecht velvet. Although seats could stray from room to room, as we see in the Choiseul box (fig. 20),[32] this inordinate number is inconsistent both with the usual activities of the Salon and with the decorative harmony we associate with French eighteenth-century interiors. Bonnet, researching this conundrum in the Archives Nationales, determined that the next-door antechamber, the *salle du dais*, was upholstered in crimson. As that antechamber was empty at the time of the 1790 inventory, it is reasonable to assume that the twenty-two seats upholstered in crimson Utrecht velvet were from the *salle du dais* rather than the Salon. Since the inventory was made after the death of the duchesse de La Trémoille, in July 1790, who had emigrated the previous year, the house evidently had been unoccupied, judging from the *housses* (covers) draped over all the furnishings. The Salon, it appears, had been used as a storeroom. In this case, not counting the unmatched chairs, one can deduce that the seating that actually belonged to the Salon amounted to nineteen seats of the *mobilier d'architecture* (the formal furniture arranged along the walls) and ten *sièges d'usage* (chairs for use rather than for display). Twenty-nine, rather than fifty-one, is a far more believable number of seats for the Salon, and it is reassuring that the upholstery's color scheme—all in blue and white, matching the curtains—was more harmonious than the inventory initially suggested.

We now understand that in a house run by a bevy of servants, the Salon was reconfigured according to the function and time of the day: formally set with two rows of seats (see fig. 21) or with the *chaises courantes* arranged in a conversational grouping around the chimneypiece for visitors in

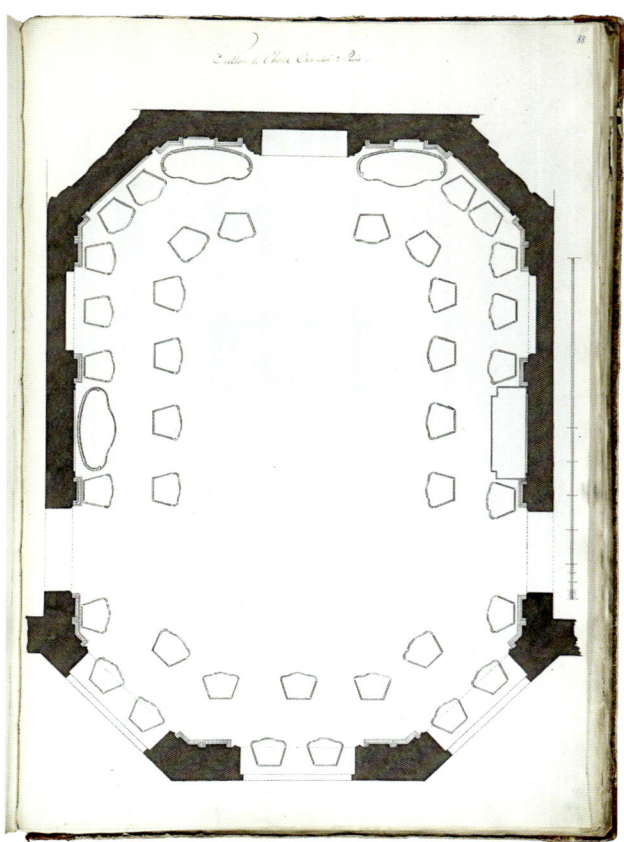

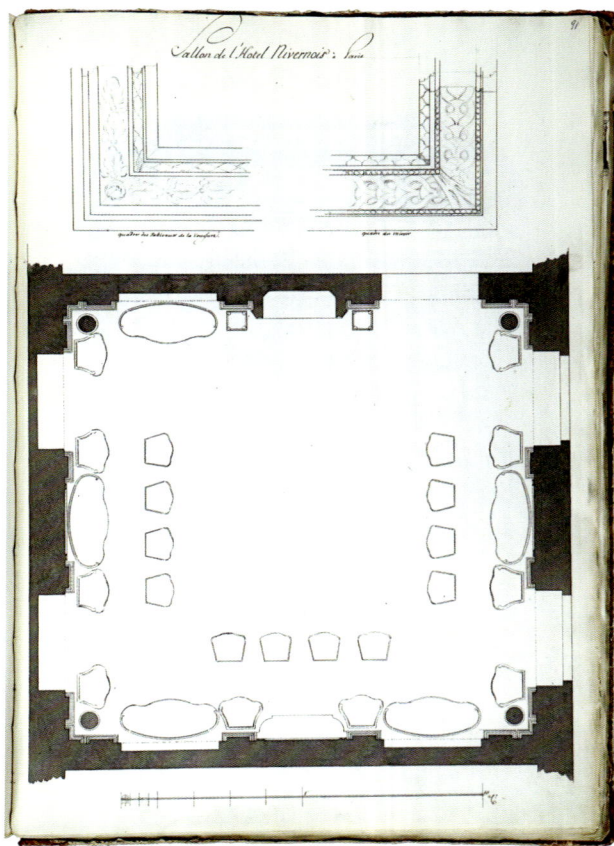

the late afternoon (see fig. 22). Both arrangements are seen in plans dated to 1778–1780, drawn by a Swedish architect, Erik Palmstedt, who recorded how Parisian salons were arranged—or deconstructed, as we see in a print of the day, with tables brought in for card games or trictrac (see fig. 23). The set of four *voyeuses* (kneeling chairs) described in the 1790 inventory was used for watching the progress of the games and gambling, both of which were important activities in the Salon; the duc de La Trémoille lamented his losses at the table, and his son the prince de Tarente apparently fared even worse, losing substantial sums.[33]

Although the inventory is not entirely reliable concerning the daily use of the Salon at its peak, it has helped us to understand far more accurately the color and composition of its furnishings. It has also informed our reconstruction of the room and provided a deeper knowledge of how its occupants arranged and used this Salon. With it, and Pons's discovery of the paneling's earlier provenance, we can more easily envision the Salon as the most splendid of the formal rooms in the *appartement de société*. With its gilded paneling and costly set of mirrors—surmounted by gilded trophies and flanked with gilded pilasters—and handsome architectural door cases with overdoors of nymphs representing Love, it speaks eloquently of the status of the La Trémoilles and the role of this room as the primary reception space in the house.

FIG. 21 (*above left*). Erik Palmstedt (Swedish, 1741–1803), floor plan of the Hôtel du Châtelet, Paris, showing the two-row circular configuration of seating, 1778–1780. Pen and ink, 20¼ × 13¾ in. (51.4 × 35 cm). Kungliga Akademien för de fria konsterna / Royal Swedish Academy of Fine Arts.

FIG. 22 (*left*). Erik Palmstedt (Swedish, 1741–1803), floor plan of the Hôtel du Nivernais, Paris, showing the U-shaped grouping of side chairs, 1778–1780. Pen and ink with pencil, 20 1/16 × 14 3/16 (51 × 36 cm). Kungliga Akademien för de fria konsterna / Royal Swedish Academy of Fine Arts.

FIG. 23. François Dequevauviller (French, 1745–1807), after Niklas Lafrensen II (Swedish, 1737–1807), *L'assemblé au salon* (*Gathering in a Salon*) (detail), 1783. Engraving and etching, 15⅞ × 19¾ in. (40.3 × 50.2 cm). Fine Arts Museums of San Francisco, museum purchase, Achenbach Foundation for Graphic Arts Endowment Fund, 1964.142.101. This view shows the salon in the Hôtel de Luynes in use during the daytime. The formal placement of the chairs has been rearranged for playing games—trictrac on the left and cards on the right—and reading by the window and conversation by the chimneypiece.

NOTES

1 John Harris, *Moving Rooms: The Trade in Architectural Salvages* (New Haven and London, 2007), 187–190. Two other *boiseries* were acquired in these years: the Louis XIV cabinet from the Carolands and some Louis XVI paneling given by Mr. James Osgood, both of which were installed near the Salon in the Legion's Gallery 7 in the early 1960s.

2 Sadly, no documentation of how Wellington discovered this provenance has been found.

3 Getty Research Institute (GRI), Duveen Brothers Records, 1876–1981. The records provide a detailed view of the business activities of Duveen Brothers (notable art dealers from the late nineteenth to the early twentieth centuries) in London, Paris, and New York. Although the archive extends from 1876 to 1981, the bulk of the material dates from Joseph Duveen's tenure as president of the firm (1909–1939) and Edward Fowles's leadership (1939–1964, with Armand Lowengard until 1943). The mass of documents, such as cables and letters, invoices, and ledgers and stock books, gives a day-by-day account of art dealing, business strategy, and the individuals involved. Included are some records from the Kleinberger Galleries (1906–1971) and Edward Fowles's papers (number 960015 969915). Fowles's correspondence with Richard Rheem, 1954–1956,

Box 498, Folders 3–4; Fowles's correspondence with Walter Heil, director of the M. H. de Young Memorial Museum, November 1953–January 1961, Box 285, Folder 6; Fowles's correspondence with Thomas Carr Howe, director of the California Palace of the Legion of Honor, November 1954–May 1960, Box 342, Folders 1–10.

4 GRI, Duveen Brothers Records, 1876–1981, letter from E. Fowles to Richard S. Rheem, March 2, 1955. The eventual cost of the room on May 1, 1956, was $77,393.02.

5 GRI, Duveen Brothers Records, Rheem, 1955, correspondence with Pierre Decour, Box 499, Folders 1 and 5, and Box 500, Folder 1.

6 GRI, Duveen Brothers Records, 1954, Duveen to M. H. de Young Memorial Museum. A memo from Fowles dated September 24, 1954, notes that Walter Heil, director of the M. H. de Young Memorial Museum, shows interest in the Crillon Room for "someone" (possibly Rheem, who was a trustee) and that he (Fowles) is sending the maquette. A letter of September 28, 1954, from Fowles to Heil confirms sending the maquette.

7 GRI, Duveen Brothers Records, letter from Fowles to Heil, December 17, 1958.

8 GRI, Duveen Brothers Records, letter from Fowles to Heil, September 28, 1954.

9 GRI, Duveen Brothers Records, letter from Fowles to Dr. James Rorimer, director of the Metropolitan Museum of Art, New York, September 19, 1958. The Hillingdon collection was a significant holding of French eighteenth-century furniture and porcelain formed by Sir Charles Mills of the London bank Glyn, Mills, and Co., which was sold by his grandson, the 3rd Lord Hillingdon, to Duveen in 1936.

10 Ibid.

11 GRI, Duveen Brothers Records, letter from Fowles to Heil, September 28, 1954. Fowles continues to Heil that the size is "just under 40 feet and the width 23 ft. 2 in. and height 14 ft. 11 in.; practically 15 feet to the cornice. It would be nice if you could leave about 2 feet for the cornice and the cove, because that's how it was in the house originally, but we hadn't sufficient height in our building to use it."

12 GRI, Duveen Brothers Records, letter from Fowles to Heil, September 4, 1957, mentioned as 24 × 27½ feet.

13 GRI, Carlhian Records, Box 744, Folder 13. The Salon is mentioned several times from 1916 to 1918 in the Carlhian correspondence on the Otto Kahn house project. Memo 17, January 27, 1916, mentions the Salon and where they were to place the old *boiserie*. Memo 837, April 28, 1916, says they are to take over the antique *boiserie* that is in the hands of the decorator Alavoine. May 26, 1916: ". . . nous devons aussi arranger son Salon Louis XVI ancien" (". . . we have to arrange her [Mrs. Kahn's] antique Louis XVI salon"). November 26, 1916, concerns Otto Kahn's house and a question of adjusting an old *boiserie*. January 31, 1918: a representative in the Paris office discusses a chandelier and wall lights, and concludes that "nous complétons la decoration des son salon, et nous attendons avec impatience l'étoffe pour ses rideaux" ("we are in the process of completing the decoration of her salon, and we are looking forward to seeing the fabric for the curtains").

14 Mairie du 7ème arrondissement, Paris, *Bulletin de la Société d'histoire et d'archéologie du VIIe arrondissement de Paris*, no. 1 (March 1906): 13.

15 Ibid., 15, 16, 17. The courtyard was much reduced in size and alterations were made by the architect Henri-Joseph-Aubert Parent (1819–1895).

16 According to the bulletin cited in n. 14, more than thirty photos of the house were taken by MM. Moreau Frères just before the demolition in 1905, and most formed part of the archives of the Société d'histoire et d'archéologie du VIIe arrondissement.

17 *La rue de Lille: Hôtel de Salm* (Paris, 1983), 65.

18 Bruno Pons, *Architecture and Panelling: The James A. de Rothschild Bequest at Waddesdon Manor* (London, 1996). The author is grateful to Ulrich Leben, curator at Waddesdon, for pointing out this fact.

19 Ibid., 408–419. Pons cited Alfred de Champeaux, *L'art decorative dans le vieux Paris, 1898* (Paris, 1898), as the source for this notion.

20 Louise-Emmanuelle de Châtillon de La Trémoille Tarente, *Souvenirs de la princesse de Tarente, 1789–1792* (Nantes, 1897; Paris, 1901), 229–242.

21 Winifred Stephens Whale, *The La Trémoille Family* (Boston and New York, 1914), 275–276. Bruno Pons cites the unpublished memoirs of the prince in *Le faubourg Saint-Germain: La rue Saint-Dominique: Hôtels et amateurs* (Paris, 1984), 69, where Tarente describes his first wife as "maigre et peu formée, d'une physionomie sauvage et peu acceuillante qui ne me plaisant du tout, mais qui plus tard finit par devenir ce qu'on appellee une belle femme" ("thin and undeveloped, with a wild look and ungracious, which did not please me at all, but later became what one calls a beautiful woman").

22 Ibid., 287.

23 It is possible that the La Trémoilles and the Tarentes may have shared the house (see *Le faubourg Saint-Germain*), but this has not been verified in the current research undertaken by Xavier Bonnet at the Archives Nationales, Paris.

24 Ibid., 69.

25 Delapoize rented space in the other Hôtel de La Trémoille on rue de Vaugirard and is mentioned as one of the architects responsible for demolishing the Bastille during the Revolution. He may have been the La Trémoille in-house architect.

26 Pons, *Architecture and Panelling*, 408–419; *Le faubourg Saint-Germain*, 68–72.

27 Archives Nationales, Paris, Inventory of the Hôtel de La Trémoille, rue Saint-Dominique, July 22, 1790, taken after the death of the duchesse de La Trémoille (see pp. 97–99 in this volume). The mirrors are described as follows: "A l'égard d'une glace de cheminée en deux parties . . . ainsi que la boiserie faisant le pourtour du dit salon . . . il n'été du tout fait aucune prisée à la réquisition des parties et du dit sieur substitut comme étant posés à perpétuelle demeure et adhérant a l'hôtel pourquoi le présent article est ici tiré pour mémoire, ci" ("With respect to a fireplace mirror in two parts . . . as well as the wood paneling along the perimeter of said salon . . . no appraisal at all has been made at the request of the parties and of said *sieur substitut* [proxy for the duke or duke's representative] as their being permanently installed and attached to the *hôtel*, on account of which the present article is recorded here for reference").

28 The furniture and effects were sold from "173 rue Dominique" for 63,915 *livres*, 3 *sols* in 1794; see Louis La Trémoille et al., *Souvenirs de la révolution: Mes parents* (Paris, 1901), 10.

29 "Cornice ornée de modillon frises et moulures sculptées et dorées dans son pou[r]tour d'un lambris d'Appui et d'hauteur à panneaux avec pilaster d'ordre Corinthien cannelé sculpté et doré, trois parquets de glaces avec archivoltes ornées de caissons et rosaces dorées, quatre portes à placards idem à deux vantaux bas reliefs au-dessus, un chambranle de cheminée en marbre blanc orné de bronzes dorés" ("Cornice decorated with modillions, frieze and moldings carved and gilded, set into its surroundings of paneling composed of a wainscot with panels above, with fluted, carved, and gilded Corinthian pilasters, three mirror parquets with archivolts [undersides of arches] decorated with gilded coffering and rosettes, four door cases with two doors each, low reliefs above, a chimneypiece in white marble decorated with gilt bronzes"). Vincennes, Archives de l'Inspection du Génie, Article 8, Paris, "Hôtels divers"; cited in Pons, *Architecture and Panelling*, 415, n33.

30 Archives Nationales, Paris, T//1051/55, *Papiers La Trémoille*. The author is grateful to Xavier Bonnet for discovering this detailed document, which describes the consoles.

31 Bruno Pons, *French Period Rooms, 1650–1800: Rebuilt in England, France, and the Americas* (Dijon, 1995), 328.

32 Ibid., 145.

33 *Le faubourg Saint-Germain*, 70; and Whale, *The La Trémoille Family*, 275–276.

LIFE IN THE SALON

Precedences, Customs, and Furnishings
in the *Appartement de Réception* of
Eighteenth-Century Parisian *Hôtels*

Alexandre Pradère

Since the Goncourt brothers, generations of eighteenth-century aficionados have aspired to dwell in homes from the times of Louis XV and Louis XVI, or amid their luxurious decors and furnishings, with the illusion that they were exactly re-creating the art of living in this golden age. That, however, is wishful thinking, as in many cases their re-creations could not have been further from the lifestyles they wished to emulate or from the original uses of these antique furnishings. The rigid caste society of the *ancien régime* (Old Regime) had completely vanished by the end of the nineteenth century, taking with it the etiquette and choreography for which those decors and furnishings were just the backdrops and the props.

THE HIERARCHY OF THE RECEPTION ROOMS

The strict hierarchy that dominated Old Regime French society likewise effectively governed the reception rooms (a specific suite of rooms then called the *appartement de société* or the *appartement de représentation*),[1] dictating the ways in which the space was occupied and its different uses (service, reception, or privacy), its distribution of light and sources of heat, and, of course, the furnishing of the salons. This hierarchy was marked by a progressive increase of richness, light, and heat, starting with the entry vestibule and ending with the formal bedchamber or the salon. Thus, along with the progression of richness came a progression of lighting, from the vestibule, dimly lit by a glass lantern; to the antechambers, lit by a single pair of wall lights; to the salon, illuminated both by a chandelier and by several pairs of gilt-bronze wall lights with candles reflected in the large mirrors that were set above the chimneypiece, on the opposite wall, and on the pier between the windows. These chandeliers were preferably made of rock crystal in the salons, while gilt-bronze chandeliers were reserved—in the opinion of the connoisseurs—to collectors' cabinets. In a sales catalogue from 1756, the expert and dealer Pierre

Remy writes: "Although [rock] crystal chandeliers have until now prevailed in the decoration of the *appartements* owing to their perfect harmony with the mirrors, which are the rooms' greatest ornament today, gilt-bronze chandeliers are, nonetheless, more noble and better suited to the *cabinets*, in which one should avoid, as much as possible, placing mirrors in the spaces that are intended for paintings."[2]

In a private Parisian mansion, a couple did not share an *appartement* (suite), and even less a bedroom, with the exception of certain financiers and their wives, such as the Labordes or the Hocquarts, who retained the bourgeois custom of sharing a room. The aristocratic model was to occupy two separate stories of the house, with the wife generally living in the *appartement du bel étage*—the second story of the main building, between the courtyard and the garden—which became the house's main reception suite (*appartement de réception*), while the husband lived on the ground floor.[3] The *appartement* unfolded from one or several antechambers where service staff were stationed, both the household's valets and those who attended visitors. A great number of household valets could be employed in princely homes; in opulent dwellings, the minimum was two or three. For example, the president of the Parlement Germain Louis Chauvelin had three footmen of his own and three more for his wife.

Opening onto the entry vestibule or the staircase (neither of which was heated), the antechambers were protected from drafts by double doors made of wooden structures covered in fabric (wool or velvet with brass nail heads) and were heated by cast-iron or earthenware stoves. There were no rich fabrics on the walls—only embossed leather wall hangings from Malines in Belgium,[4] wood paneling, or verdure tapestries—and there were no curtains on the windows. The furnishing of the antechambers, always very sober, included benches or chairs, painted or unpainted, covered in sturdy materials, such as moquette (thick pile velvet), needlepoint, stamped velvet, leather, or horsehair, that would not absorb odors, since these rooms often served as dining rooms. Coffers in the form of low sideboards contained mattresses that were pulled out for the footmen to sleep on at night. Other low sideboards were used for meal service, with stoneware or copper fountains for hand washing, while *armoires* built into the paneling often held dishes and glassware.

The antechambers were, as noted above, used as dining rooms. Generally there was no fixed dining table—such tables would become fashionable only through British influence in the 1780s—but simply tabletops made of pine that would be placed on oak trestles at mealtimes, while the rest of the time they remained either behind large folding screens in the antechamber itself or in the staircase hall. These screens also hid other small, lightweight furnishings (writing tables, *chiffonières*, gaming tables) that the servants would carry into the salons as an occasion demanded. Large houses might have two antechambers, one to be used by the servants (*les gens*) and the other by noble visitors (*les seigneurs*), and in that case the second antechamber was richer, sometimes even furnished in giltwood and, as at the Hôtel de Noailles on rue Saint-Honoré, sumptuous furniture by André-Charles Boulle.

In ducal residences, the *appartement de réception*

was doubled by a more formal suite (a state apartment), further including an *antichambre du dais*, a room dominated by a canopy embroidered with the family's coat of arms.⁵ Next came the true reception room, which was the formal bedchamber of the mistress (or master) of the house, generally hung with crimson damask and dominated by a large bed. The same silks would be used as wall hangings and on the numerous seats in the room (it was not rare to have up to thirty or so). This room had no intimate nature but instead served as the salon, often extended by a private bedroom of smaller dimensions that was easier to heat in winter. Only beyond this room did the owners' private quarters begin, namely, the *appartement de commodité* (convenience suite), boudoir, and *cabinet de toilette* (dressing room) for the woman and the library and *cabinet de travail* (study) for the man—rooms reserved for private life, generously furnished and filled with personal objects or collection pieces.

Cabinetwork was concentrated largely in the private rooms, while the salons were principally furnished in giltwood. At the Palais Royal in 1724, the Hôtel de Noailles in 1739, and the Hôtel de Toulouse in 1744,⁶ the salons contained only giltwood seats and console tables. These console tables were placed beneath the pier mirrors that were always found between the windows and directly across from the chimneypiece mirror and sometimes on the far wall facing the windows. Commodes, considered storage furniture (and, as such, placed in private bedrooms, dressing rooms, and private sitting rooms), were almost never found in salons before 1750. Beginning in the 1760s, this trend changed. At that point more and more space in the salons was given over to cabinetwork—corner cupboards and commodes of lacquerwork or marquetry—at the expense of the giltwood console tables of previous decades. Thus, one would find at Versailles a porcelain-mounted commode by Carlin in the comtesse du Barry's salon and, in Marie-Antoinette's *salon des nobles*, a series of three mahogany commodes by Jean-Henri Riesener, or, in the salon of the *fermier-général* Claude Dupin in 1769, two commodes in place of the usual giltwood console tables.⁷

In large houses, the formal bedchamber tended more and more to be preceded by another reception room called the *salon d'assemblée, salon de compagnie*, or *grand cabinet*. These new rooms were the salons that over the course of the eighteenth century gradually came to replace the formal bedchambers in their richness and their representative role; they became synonymous with the art of living in the Old Regime.

For the most part, the furnishing of these salons did not express the personalities of their owners; there were usually no personal objects, books, family portraits or miniatures, or collection pieces besides decorative large-format paintings, numerous porcelains arranged on the mantel, and occasionally some bronze pieces. The decor and its expensive materials (giltwood, gilt bronzes, rich silks, rock-crystal chandeliers) reflected, above all, the social status of its occupants but remained perfectly impersonal. At the Marshal de Belle-Isle's *hôtel*, in 1761, the large salon on the quai d'Orsay was adorned with mirrors on all four walls that reflected the Parisian sky and view of the Seine through windows on two walls, with the only furniture being a large sofa and ten armchairs made of giltwood with green-painted highlights and covered in green, red, and white Genoa velvet. The sumptuous lighting included *girandoles aux enfants* (candelabra modeled with children) fixed to the chimneypiece by their bases, and four candelabra with figures in Meissen porcelain placed on the console tables between the windows. Forty years later, the second duc de Choiseul-Praslin converted this *salon d'assemblée* into a *cabinet de collectionneur*. The mirrors were then replaced by wall hangings of green fabric on which numerous Flemish and Dutch paintings were hung. The console tables between the windows were replaced by small cabinets made of Japanese lacquerwork, the large sofa was exchanged for a commode by Boulle decorated with winged women, and the other walls received armoires by Boulle surmounted by vases of precious marble.

The richness of the interiors was restrained, in relation to the social status of its occupants, by a principle then known as *bienséance* (decorum). Nonetheless, the residences of financiers were often more sumptuous than those of great lords, especially in the countryside. In her short treatise on good manners (inspired by the dictums of the Marshal de Luxembourg's wife, "l'oracle du bon ton"—the oracle of good taste—in Paris), Mme de Genlis thus opposed selfish bourgeois luxury (sumptuous interiors) to "the spirit of magnificence," that is, aristocratic splendor (masses of servants and numerous horses and carriages), which was intended to be shared:

> The spirit of magnificence had a solid and beneficial quality. The selfish magnificence of pure ostentation seemed in poor taste. For example, all the great lords and princes of royal blood furnished their chateaux and pleasure palaces in the most modest simplicity . . . while the bankers displayed the most brilliant ostentation in their country homes. But the princes and great lords availed themselves of extreme luxury in anything that might afford enjoyment to others—horses and carriages; open banquets; lodging in their palaces, even for people who had no connection to their house; parties; theater boxes that they endlessly lent to their friends; and finally, servants, which were far more numerous than they are today.[8]

FURNISHINGS AND CUSTOMS IN THE SALON

Salons had two types of seating, each with its own arrangement: formal seats, called *sièges meublants*, consisting of sofas and large armchairs with flat backs, often in giltwood, placed along the walls around the room; and more utilitarian seats, or *sièges courants*, sometimes called *coureurs* (meaning "runners" or "running" chairs), which were the chairs and cabriolet armchairs (chairs with slightly rounded backs) that were lighter and easier to move, and used to form a circle or an oval at the center of the room.[9] In princely houses, the *sièges meublants* were solely decorative pieces, as Mme de Genlis explained: "In the *appartements* [of princes], one was not supposed to sit in the armchairs or on the sofas. The armchairs were merely decorative, their backs set against the paneling. There were rows of chairs with large backs for company. The princess had an armchair but, apart from using it for introductions, she never sat in it."[10]

FIG. 24. Jean François de Troy (French, 1679–1752), *The Reading from Molière*, ca. 1728. Oil on canvas, 28½ × 35¾ in. (72.4 × 90.8 cm). Private collection.

Bergères (comfortable armchairs with deep seat cushions and padded sides) or *fauteuils de commodité* (low, comfortable armchairs with little apparent wood), such as those seen in Jean François de Troy's famous painting *The Reading from Molière* (fig. 24), were arranged on both sides of the fireplace. Those seated in them were shielded from drafts by folding screens and sheltered from the intensity of the fire by multiple screens in wooden frames (there were sometimes two or three in each salon, some having three or four leaves) or paper hand screens. The mistress of the house, particularly if she was older, would sit next to the fire, in one of the *bergères*. The ladies would sit in a circle around her, with the older ones closest to the fire. No one sat directly in front of the fireplace, since that would block the heat for those sitting farther away. Most of the men remained standing. At the home of the duchesse de Gramont, the duc de Choiseul's sister, she and the wife of the Marshal

FIG. 25. Unknown artist (French, nineteenth century), salon from the Hôtel de Beauvau, Paris, 1805. Private collection. This illustration shows the *cercle* around the fireplace, with the maréchale de Beauvau and the old duc de Chabot near the fire; the family circle of the Noailles, Beauvau, and Rohan ladies seated; and the younger men standing.

de Luxembourg were customarily seated on either side of the fireplace, with the men standing in a circle between them, as a contemporary related.

An interior view of the salon of the Marshal de Beauvau's wife, situated on the *entresol* (the smaller living floor usually situated between the first and second floors), shows the marshal's wife comfortably seated beside the fire with a circle of ladies around her, while the old duc de Chabot stands in front of the hearth to warm himself, a privilege of his advanced age (fig. 25). The older men are seated, but the younger men remain standing, away from the flames. Mme de Genlis recalls that at Versailles, during the gaming sessions held by the queen in her apartments, "the men would make their court to the sovereign. . . . Those who were not playing stayed standing, no matter what their rank, in keeping with the established etiquette of French gallantry."[11]

The custom of the circle (see fig. 26) made it necessary for those arriving to enter discreetly. Here, too, Mme de Genlis describes these furtive ballets:

> Of all the new practices [this text was written in ca. 1812–1813], the manner of entering a circle and leaving it is the one that differs most from older customs. Formerly one would enter the salon with a slow, measured stride, a modest bearing, [and] would quietly take the nearest available seat. The mistress of the house would give her greeting with-

out leaving her seat and would address a few words in an obliging tone to the new arrival. When the circle was not too large, she would go up to the person and greet them with kisses, and then return to her place. After the visit, one would attempt to leave furtively, seizing the moment when others were entering; usually the mistress of the house would pretend not to notice this departure, to avoid the awkwardness of seeing the person out.[12]

The baron de Frénilly, another talented memorialist, recounts the difficulty of these entries, which necessitated actual etiquette lessons:

> A young man's entry into society thus required thorough study, constituting the final course of education, after philosophy and the humanities. It was no meager skill to enter with grace and assurance a salon where thirty men and women were seated in a circle

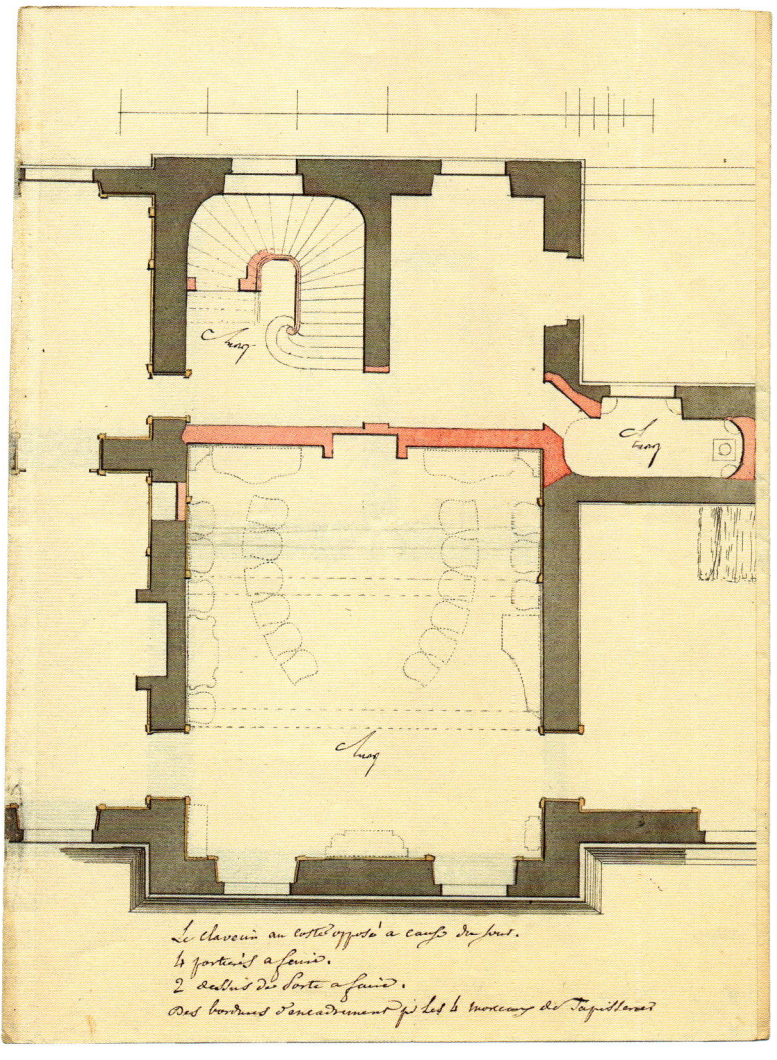

FIG. 26. Plan detailing the arrangement of the Salon d'Hiver in the Château de Ménars, annotated by the marquis de Marigny. Pen, ink, and watercolor.

around the fire, to move into the circle while nimbly greeting all those around, to make one's way to the mistress of the house, and to withdraw honorably, managing without awkwardness a dress coat, lace, a coiffure of thirty-six curls powdered like snow, a hat under one arm, a sword whose point touched one heel, and finally, an enormous muff.... I took a month of lessons from the celebrated Petit, at twelve francs a session, for this part of my education.[13]

The rules of society life had not completely changed in the nineteenth century, when baronne Staffe described, in her delectable treatise on good manners, the custom of the circle in front of the fireplace:

> The lady of the house is seated at one corner of the fireplace. She turns her back to the windows. This spot, which is not very advantageous for beauty, is hers precisely for this reason, because in her home she must highlight all the talents and qualities of others and efface herself completely. They form a large half-circle. The old women are seated closest to the fire. Should a young woman be sitting there when an older woman arrives, she discreetly slides into another chair. The young people must make sure they never remain seated above the old people, that is, closer to the fire. In some houses, guests are announced. In others, a servant (whether a footman or a simple maid) opens the door for the visitor without saying a word. The visitor then goes up to the mistress of the house, who remains seated if it is a man who introduces himself but rises and takes two steps forward if it is a woman.[14]

This notion of warmth remained relative and was certainly far removed from modern criteria: in the mid-nineteenth century, when heating conditions had not changed, fifty-five degrees (Fahrenheit) was considered sufficiently warm for a dining room in the winter.[15]

Furthermore, to understand the furnishing of these salons (and particularly the absence of small tables), it is important to realize that no food or beverages were served in them. The custom of serving refreshments or aperitifs was completely unknown in salon life. "When not at the table, if someone was thirsty and asked for a drink, they had to go drink in the antechamber. It was absolutely impolite to drink in the salon," Mme de Genlis explains. The custom of serving sorbet as a light refreshment also did not emerge until under the Napoleonic Empire, as Frénilly notes: "Certain people had regular days [for entertaining]. It was not yet the fashion to eat ices standing up, treading on each other's toes."[16]

Although the opera (or the theater) played an important role as an early evening activity at that time, the afternoon round of visits and the circle of conversation structured social life. Frénilly writes:

> Performances were not, as in Italy and part of Germany, the obligatory evening occupation. There were many pleasant circles where the mistress of the house remained home [to entertain], either all the time or on set days. And what superior talent these hostesses dis-

played! . . . Captivating their guests; directing, prolonging, resuming, or shortening a conversation; having a look, a word, for each person; drawing an outsider, by a mere glance or word, into the friendly conversation of others; bringing that person into contact with them and enabling them to recognize him without names or introductions—what a charming, delicate art![17]

These visits were an obligation that few could escape, according to Moravan de Bellegarde: "Most people of quality, who are ordinarily quite idle and have no occupation, pass their time paying or receiving visits."[18] The visits took place in the late afternoon for those who were not going to the theater, and they ended at suppertime, as Lady Crewe, an Englishwoman passing through Paris in 1786, remarked: "At five o'clock in the afternoon, everyone goes out to visit everyone else."[19]

In certain salons, music was the center of interest, such as at the home of the *fermier-général* Alexandre Leriche de La Pouplinière, who retained fifteen musicians in 1762. The Sunday gatherings at his Château de Passy followed an unchanging ritual: a mass in music followed by a large luncheon. Afterward, people would chat and play chess; then at five o'clock a concert would be given in the second-floor gallery with a sizable audience from Paris. Supper was served at nine o'clock, and finally there would be another concert, for close friends.[20]

Along with conversation and music, games were another activity that filled society life, requiring the presence of numerous gaming tables in the salon (see fig. 27). These tables, generally

FIG. 27. Jean-Baptiste Mallet (French, 1759–1835), *L'assemblée au salon*, ca. 1790. Hand-colored engraving. Private collection. This illustration shows a view of the grand salon of the Hôtel de Luynes.

FIG. 28. Nicolas Delaunay (French, 1739–1792), *Le billet doux* (*The Love Letter*) (detail), 1778. Line engraving, 18⅜ × 13⁹⁄₁₆ in. (46.8 × 34.4 cm). Fine Arts Museums of San Francisco, gift of Archer M. Huntington, 1927.310. In this image one can see the mistress of the house sitting next to the fireplace, but the portrait and the carpet indicate that this is a room in the private apartments rather than a *salon de compagnie*.

of cherrywood covered in green cloth, were often foldable and preferably stored in the antechamber, to be carried in by servants. Their quantity, and the number of reception guests and players, dictated the need for small seats, stools, or *voyeuses* (kneeling chairs with low seats and high backs), allowing guests to follow the game more comfortably. On the place of games in social life, Mme de la Briche wrote from Dijon in 1808: "The house we are living in, which is vast, is completely packed [during receptions] . . . on Mondays, out of fifty people, forty-five are playing; every two weeks, my daughter gives a ball, which enchants the young people."[21] The large number of guests frequently received in the salons obviously explains the great many seats described in the inventories, but it also explains the impersonal nature of these reception rooms. In her memoirs, Mme de La Tour du Pin recalls equally large gatherings when she accompanied her uncle, who presided over the Estates of Languedoc, to Montpellier: "We had to be dressed and in all our finery by exactly three o'clock for dinner. We'd go up to the salon, where we would find fifty guests every day."[22]

SUPPERS IN TOWN

Some of the great Parisian hostesses often remained at home to receive visits both afternoon and evening, such as Mme Geoffrin, who never went out. Others had a fixed day to receive visitors for a conversation circle or a supper, although whether these suppers were by invitation or were open banquets for a group of regulars is not clear. In most of the great houses, in fact, a tradition of open banquets existed. According to Bombelles, "There is no great house where one is not adequately set up to serve a table of a hundred places. Every Monday, the baron de Breteuil gives a supper for even more guests, and his kitchens are perfectly sufficient."[23]

Mme du Deffant served three weekly suppers in her home. The duc de Biron gave a supper every Friday for forty-some guests in his mansion on rue de Varenne (which now houses the Musée Rodin). Such was also the case at the Palais Royal on certain days of the week for those who had been formally introduced, and likewise at the duc de Choiseul's home in Versailles in 1758, as Dufort de Cheverny recounts: "During that time, one would dine [have lunch] at exactly two o'clock; all the foreigners who had been formally introduced were admitted, as well as all the courtiers; the large table had thirty-five places set, and another equally large table stood at the ready, although one did not see it. A valet would count the guests as they entered, and as soon as the number exceeded thirty-five, the other table was set accordingly, fully served apart."[24]

Sometimes the mistress of the house would have a valet inform certain visitors that they were asked to stay for supper, as Dufort de Cheverny also recalls: "I was in the habit of going for supper every Monday at the home of the duchesse de Praslin, where the whole court could be found, as well as the ambassadors.... As soon as you arrived, a valet in the second antechamber would invite you on behalf of the duchess to stay for supper. We would play a *brelan à cinq* [a five-person card game].... This went on through the night, until three o'clock in the morning; at that point those who were not regulars would leave."[25]

Because both opera and theater performances took place in the late afternoon, the mealtimes that organized society life grew later and later over the course of the eighteenth century. Lunch (which was then called "dinner" [*dîner*]) had long been served around two o'clock, and supper around nine. In the 1780s, the French came to adopt Spanish mealtimes: two or three o'clock for dinner and ten o'clock for supper. According to Mme de La Tour du Pin:

> During that period there were never any great dinner parties [luncheons]. The women sometimes had their hair done, but they were never dressed up for dinner because people dined early, at half-past two or three o'clock at the latest. The men were almost always in formal attire ... after dinner, people would chat; sometimes they would play a game of trictrac [an early form of backgammon]. The women would go get dressed, while the men waited so they could accompany them to the performance if they had seats in the same box. If they stayed home after dinner, there would be a steady stream of visitors. Only at nine-thirty would the supper guests arrive.[26]

On the daily schedule of social life during the 1780s, the information we have from baron de Frénilly complements that of Mme de La Tour du Pin: "People dined [lunched] at two o'clock and supped at ten. The dinners were formal, and the suppers were for pleasure. They had supper after the performance, which began between five and six and ended between eight and nine.... Games, conversation, and laughter prolonged the festivities until two o'clock in the morning. The only occupation was pleasure. One would get up late [the next day]."²⁷

An Alsatian woman traveling through Paris in 1782 in the retinue of the comtesse du Nord (Marie Feodorovna, Grand Duchess Paul of Russia) noted the rapid pace of dinners (lunches): "They dine at three o'clock, and the dinners have become very quick, a fact that gourmets and conversationalists loudly lament. . . . Supper is at ten o'clock and is just as rushed. Meals are no longer announced: when it is time to sit at the table, the butler appears and the mistress rises to her feet. The age of gourmandise has passed. For all that, the tables are no less sumptuously laid. The luxury is terrifying."²⁸

The guests' passage from the salon to the dining room and the seating at the table followed different rules from those that would be customary in the nineteenth century. There was no procession, no male/female alternation as would become common at the end of the nineteenth century, and no formal table seating (except at court). Here again, Mme de Genlis provides details: "The men did not give the women their hand to pass into the dining room, except outside of Paris. In Paris this practice was never seen at either suppers or dinners. There, all the women would go into the dining room first, in order of their proximity to the door. They would exchange a few greetings in doing so, and then all the men would follow. Everyone would take whatever place they wished at the table."²⁹

At the end of the meal, the guests would rise to perform their none-too-pleasant ablutions, as Mme de Genlis describes: "The women, after dinner or supper, would get up and leave the table to rinse their mouths; the men, out of respect for the women, did not remain in the dining room to do the same but would go to an antechamber. Today [under the Empire], this type of grooming is done at the table . . . this custom comes from England."³⁰ Thus the small vessels now decorously called "finger bowls" appeared on tables at that time.

All in all, if we compare the image we have just portrayed of salon life under the Old Regime with the present day, what has changed the most? Would it be the disappearance of caste society, of the rigid old social codes? Or the end of the civilization of idleness? Viewed solely from a decorative-arts perspective, the biggest changes are more prosaic: the reduction of service staff encouraged the specialization of spaces and the multiplication of small tables; central heating led to the loss of the circle of conversation by the fire; the custom of consuming alcoholic drinks and smoking tobacco in society imposed a new item of furniture, the low table, which filled the center of the salons, creating a perception of space completely contrary to that of the eighteenth century, when the centers of rooms were empty; and, especially, the advent of comfort. This word, unknown in France until the second half of the nineteenth century, represents a modern notion. It coincides with the appearance of chairs with springs (invented at the beginning of the Bourbon Restoration), which became widespread, together with overstuffed or padded upholstery, under Napoleon III. With the spread of these deep armchairs, which were heavier and more difficult to move around a room, the mobility that the older chairs afforded was lost. The comfort resulting from the new chairs, as well as from the progress in heating, tended to foster a state of well-being akin to drowsiness, according to some authors, that was doubtless far removed from the alert conversation of the eighteenth century. We leave it to others to settle the debate on the development of comfort and the decline of conversation.

NOTES

1. Jean-Nicolas Dufort, comte de Cheverny, *Mémoires sur le règne de Louis XV* (Paris, 1990), 170.
2. Sales catalogue of the duc de Tallard, Paris, March–May 1756 (Lugt 910).
3. However, in the Hôtel de La Trémoille, the apartments were side by side because there was not a second floor.
4. "July 13 1782. We went to Malines.... Madame the Grand Duchess bought some beautiful lace and lovely hangings in gilt leather that are made there and that are called Spanish leather." Henriette-Louise de Waldner de Freundstein, baronne d'Oberkirch, *Mémoires de la baronne d'Oberkirch sur la cour de Louis XVI* (Paris, 1970), 247.
5. There was a *salle du dais* in the Hôtel de La Trémoille. See Xavier Bonnet's essay in this volume.
6. The Hôtel de Toulouse is now the Banque de France; the Hôtel de Noailles, now demolished, was on rue Saint-Honoré, near the place Vendôme. See A. Pradère, "L'hôtel de Noailles rue Saint-Honoré de Louis XIV à la Restauration," in *Bulletin de la Société de l'Histoire de l'Art Français*, Année 2010, Paris, 2011, 85–112.
7. However, the consoles were retained in the Salon of the Hôtel de La Trémoille.
8. Stéphanie Félicité du Crest, comtesse de Genlis, *De l'esprit des étiquettes de l'ancienne cour et des usages du monde de ce temps*, written ca. 1812–1813 (Paris, 1996), 20.
9. Only two contemporary plans documenting the seating arrangements are known to exist. The Châtelet plan (see fig. 21) shows a two-row circular configuration, which was likely the way in which the *sièges courants* were arranged by the servants when the room was not in use, especially in palaces and very formal houses. The Marigny plan (see fig. 26) illustrates a circular or oval shape that indicates how the chairs were arranged for visitors for the ease of conversation and to encircle the hearth.
10. Genlis, *De l'esprit des étiquettes*, 87.
11. Ibid.
12. Ibid., 96.
13. François-Auguste, baron Fauveau de Frénilly, *Souvenirs d'un ultraroyaliste* (Paris, 1987), 17.
14. Blanche-Augustine-Angèle Soyer, baronne Staffe, *Usages du monde: règles du savoir-vivre dans la société moderne* (Paris, 1893).
15. Jules Rostaing, *Manuel de la politesse* (Paris [ca. 1870], 2012), 121.
16. Frénilly, *Souvenirs*, 249.
17. Ibid., 38.
18. Quoted in Antoine Lilti, *Le monde des salons: sociabilité et mondanité à Paris au XVIIIe siècle* (Paris, 2005), 63.
19. Handwritten journal quoted in ibid.
20. Stéphanie Félicité du Crest, comtesse de Genlis, *Mémoires inédits de madame la comtesse de Genlis, sur le dix-huitième siècle et la révolution française, depuis 1756 jusqu'à nos jours* (Paris, 1825), 1:95.
21. Quoted in Frénilly, *Souvenirs*, 254.
22. Henriette Lucy Dillon, marquise de La Tour du Pin, *Mémoires de la marquise de La Tour du Pin* (Paris, 1979), 53.
23. Marc-Marie, marquis de Bombelles, *Journal* (Geneva, 1982), 2:108.
24. De Cheverny, *Mémoires*, 253.
25. Ibid., 331.
26. La Tour du Pin, *Mémoires*, 38.
27. Frénilly, *Souvenirs*, 254.
28. Oberkirch, *Mémoires*, 310.
29. Genlis, *De l'esprit des étiquettes*, 95.
30. Ibid.

THE FURNISHINGS OF THE HÔTEL DE LA TRÉMOILLE

Xavier Bonnet

Reading the archival documents concerning the Hôtel de La Trémoille on rue Saint-Dominique, Paris, in light of a recently discovered inventory prepared in 1790 (see pp. 97–99 in this volume), after the death of the duchesse de La Trémoille, enables us to reconstruct the mansion's furnishings with new precision.[1] But before we examine such details, first let us look at the context for the habitation and use of the residence.

THE RESIDENCES OF THE DUC DE LA TRÉMOILLE

Occupied until July 1, 1781,[2] by Armand Thomas Hue, marquis de Miromesnil (1723–1796)—at that time chancellor (*garde des Sceaux*) under Louis XVI—the *hôtel* on rue Saint-Dominique (fig. 29) became the main Parisian residence of the duc and duchesse de La Trémoille following the marriage of their eldest son, the prince de

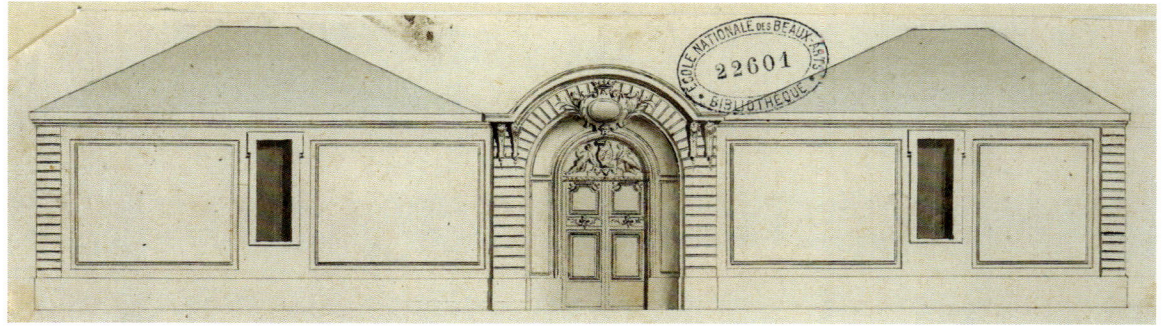

FIG. 29. Jean-Michel Chevotet (French, 1698–1772), entrance to the Hôtel Béthune (later the Hôtel de Châtillon and the Hôtel de La Trémoille). Drawing for the etching in Jacques-François Blondel, *L'Architecture françoise* (Paris, 1752–1756). École nationale supérieure des Beaux-Arts, Paris. This drawing shows the street facade of the *hôtel* on rue Saint-Dominique. This drawing has been reversed for the purposes of engraving.

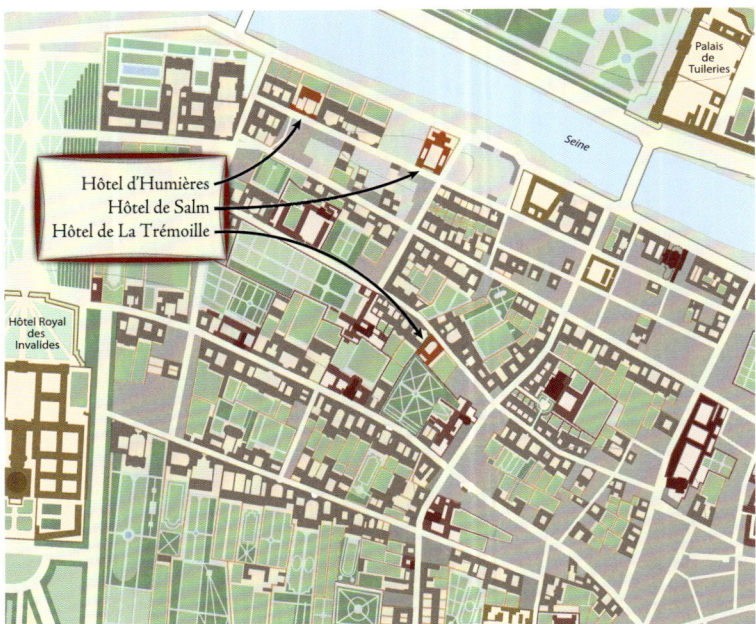

FIG. 30 (*top*). Heliogravure by Dujardin of the princesse de Tarente, from *Souvenirs de la princesse de Tarente, 1789–1792*, by Louise-Emmanuelle de Châtillon de La Trémoille Tarente (Nantes: Émile Grimaud et fils, 1897).

FIG. 31 (*bottom*). Map of the faubourg Saint-Germain, Paris, showing the locations of the Hôtel d'Humières, the Hôtel de Salm, and the Hôtel de La Trémoille in the late eighteenth century.

Tarente, to the owner of the property, Louise-Emmanuelle de Châtillon (fig. 30). Work on the residence and the purchase of furnishings immediately ensued, and the family moved in over several months, between April and September 1782.[3] Set between a courtyard and garden, this *hôtel* offered greater comfort than the family's previous residence, owned by the duke, on rue Sainte-Avoye.[4] Leaving the Marais, which had been the fashionable quarter in the seventeenth century, for the faubourg Saint-Germain (see fig. 31), the duc de La Trémoille joined the great aristocratic families who had been moving into that area over the course of the eighteenth century. By the eve of the Revolution, more than two-thirds of the dukes lived there. The duc de La Trémoille also owned a *hôtel* at the western corner of rue de Vaugirard and rue Ferou, but the family did not live in it. Under the direction of the architect Heussée (?–1782),[5] who was also the duke's *valet de chambre* (manservant), it was rebuilt in the mid-1770s by the master builder and contractor Jean-Baptiste-Nicolas Michau, who also provided the plans.[6] This *hôtel* was a rental property consisting of three suites (*appartements*), each occupying one of the main floors, and their accompanying service rooms. For brief stays during the summer months, the family had a second residence located on the outskirts of Paris, on rue de Charonne in the faubourg Saint-Antoine. From May to early November, the La Trémoilles retired to their chateau at Attichy, near Compiègne. Their stay there was rarely continuous, however, as it was interrupted by trips back and forth to Paris to attend to the demands of business or society life. Last of all, court life made it necessary for the duke to have a *hôtel* at Versailles; this *hôtel* was located on rue des Réservoirs, north of the palace of Versailles.

THE ARRANGEMENT OF THE GRANDS APPARTEMENTS

The uniqueness of the *hôtel* on rue Saint-Dominique rested on its use of a parcel of land stretching alongside the public road. The usual arrangement of the *hôtel* on a deep site between the courtyard and the garden was prevented by the neighboring Convent of the Annunciation on rue du Bac, which was immediately behind the property. Jacques-François Blondel lauded the architect, Pierre Cailleteau, known as Lassurance (1655–1724), for his ingenuity in turning this constraint to his advantage:

> The arrangement of this *hôtel* is quite ingenious, and worthy of being imitated on any parcel that has meager depth and, by contrast, extensive length. This consideration led [the architect] to place the most beautiful *appartements* on the ground floor in a wing facing the garden [see fig. 32], so that only the building at the back of the courtyard rises to three stories, its slight appearance projecting a faint notion of the importance of this house—a circumstance that sometimes forms an essential part of a building's propriety.[7]

Lassurance placed the *grands appartements* not in the *corps de logis* (main building) at the back of the courtyard but in the left wing, thus shifting the principal axis of the dwelling, as Louis Le Vau had done with the Hôtel Lambert in the mid-seventeenth century. The sobriety of the main body of the building was striking for a ducal residence: simple in mass, it had only two main floors and five bays. The central bay, crowned by a triangular pediment, opened to the interior at the ground floor, reached by five steps outside the building. These led not to the customary entry hall or grand staircase, but instead directly into the *appartement de société*, a series of three

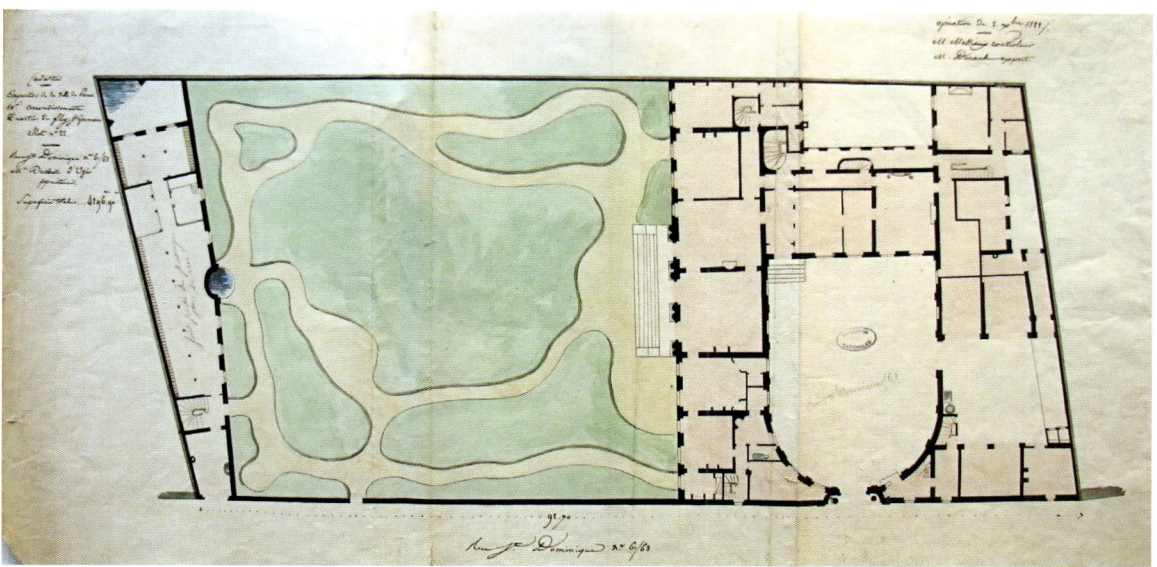

FIG. 32. Floor plan and map of the Hôtel de La Trémoille showing its unusual relationship to the garden, 1822. Archives Nationales, Paris.

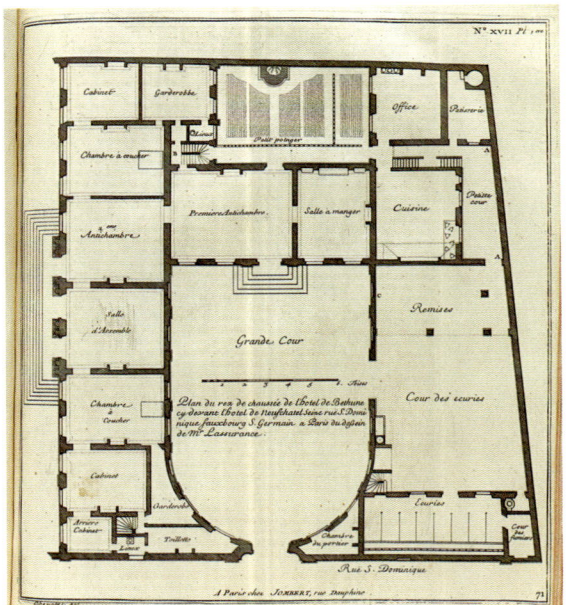

FIG. 33. Jacques-François Blondel (French, 1705–1774), plan of the Hôtel Béthune (later the Hôtel de Châtillon and the Hôtel de La Trémoille) from *L'Architecture françoise* (Paris, 1752–1756). Chateaux de Versailles et de Trianon, Versailles, France. The lower edge of the drawing represents the north-facing side of the building, with the street entrance to the courtyard in the center. The eastern side of the building, facing the garden, is at left.

One should avoid placing dining rooms, which are in constant use, within the sequence of the main *appartement*, because the time that the servants must spend performing their duties there interrupts the communication between the dining room and those rooms intended for company, and deprives the latter rooms of a view of the enfilade of rooms. Moreover, the humidity and the odor of fruits and meats during each season of the year spread too easily among all the neighboring *appartements*, tarnishing the furniture, the gilding, the bronzes, and so on.[8]

On the east side, across from the dining room, the *appartement de société* was followed by a second antechamber, which was that of the *valets de chambre* (menservants), who took over from the *valets de pieds* at this point, accompanying the visitors into the areas of the apartments that followed. At the Hôtel de La Trémoille, the second antechamber served as the *salle du dais* (audience chamber) —the room displaying a canopy embroidered with the family's coat of arms—in keeping with the protocol of ducal residences. It occupied a pivotal place in the layout of the *hôtel*, articulating the junction between the main building and the wing along the garden. This room thus linked two series of rooms: the duchess's *appartement*, to the north, and the duke's, to the south. The interiors of the duchess's *appartement* offered the features of both an *appartement d'apparat* (state apartment) and an *appartement de commodité* (private apartment), respectively. The first two rooms were used to receive guests: first the Salon (see fig. 34), with its gilding, next to the bedchamber, which took the place of a *chambre d'apparat* (state bedcham-

rooms running parallel to the facade. All these rooms were devoid of gilding, and each one was heated by an earthenware stove. The first antechamber occupied the three left-hand bays of the *corps de logis*. This is where the four *valets de pieds* (footmen) officiated, receiving guests upon arrival and leading them from the courtyard into this first room. The dining room, west of the first antechamber, was set away from the other rooms of the *appartement* in accord with the principles of utility that Blondel invokes:

FIG. 34. Jean-Michel Chevotet (French, 1698–1772), cross section of the *corps de logis* of the Hôtel Béthune (later the Hôtel de Châtillon and the Hôtel de La Trémoille). Drawing for the etching in Jacques-François Blondel, *L'Architecture françoise* (Paris, 1752–1756). École nationale supérieure des Beaux-Arts, Paris. The Salon is shown on the left with its previous configuration of paneling. This drawing has been reversed for the purposes of engraving. Here the drawing, shown in reverse, depicts the correct orientation.

ber). By contrast, the three following rooms more resembled those of an *appartement de commodité*: a library and boudoir beside the garden, and a dressing room overlooking the courtyard. The latter two rooms had lower ceilings to accommodate an *entresol* (mezzanine) that housed the duchess's servants. The atmosphere of these smaller spaces and their furnishings was decisively more intimate.

The duke's *appartement* was more sober, without gilding. It was made up of a bedroom and a small salon facing the garden, as well as a study overlooking a small back courtyard.

RENOVATING THE *HÔTEL*

Comparing the inventory made on August 16, 1780,⁹ with that of 1790 reveals extensive refurbishing of the paneling in almost every room of the ground-floor *appartements*. Changes in several elements underline the considerable scope of the project: the number of windows and bed or sofa niches; the shape, number, and dimensions of the mirrors; the shape and number of the overdoors, and their decorative subjects and techniques; and the fabric hangings. This work was carried out under the direction of Pierre-Auguste Delapoize (?–1799), the duke's appointed architect. The changes consisted essentially of replacing the rococo-style ornamentation with a decor more compatible with the contemporary Neoclassicism. Whereas thirty-six painted canvases had adorned the overdoors in 1780, there were only fourteen in 1790. Neoclassical bas-reliefs were no doubt preferred here as in the Salon. Gilding was removed from the duke's bedroom and remained only in the duchess's *appartement* (in the Salon, bedroom, and boudoir); the wall hangings that had decorated the duchess's Salon and dressing room in 1780 were also abandoned.

Though very few bills survive, some reports made by experts—pursuant to disputes that arose between the duke and his suppliers—reveal the names of those who executed changes to the fixed decor. For example, a report by the master carpenter Vincent Demazau, on rue de Provence, cites an amount of 21,719 *livres* and 7 *sols* requested for work performed in 1781 and 1782,[10] one of carving by Royer *père* mentioning joinery by Sené,[11] and a bill for painting by Henry Royer *fils*.[12]

FURNISHING THE *HÔTEL*

The duke and duchess made two of their *valets de chambres* responsible for overseeing the furnishing of the *hôtel*. The first, Heussée, died while the work was being carried out. His role seems to have been secondary to that of Antoine Vitet (1743–1788), described as the *valet de chambre tapissier*, who handled payments for most of the purchases, directed the new work, and organized the move, spending more than 40,000 *livres* between 1781 and 1783.[13] We know of only a few of the merchants and artisans used: in addition to those mentioned above, there was also the cabinetmaker Héricourt,[14] the *marchand-mercier* (dealer in works of art) Daguerre,[15] and the fabric merchant Le Normand.[16] Vitet did not engage the great *maître tapissiers* (master upholsterers) of the day, as did the duc de Coigny with Claude-François Capin or the marquis de Marigny with Charles-Henry Poussin. He made use of master upholsterers only to care for the rugs or to rent furniture (such as that rented for the wedding of the prince de Tarente or for bereavements). For furniture, he turned to two persons named Gavignet and Jourdan, neither of whom figures in the list of Parisian master upholsterers.[17] They were likely journeymen employed temporarily to furnish the duke's home. Many pieces of furniture were bought at large estate sales, such as the one held after the death of Marie-Jeanne Girardot de Vermenoux, the widow of the banker Georges Tobie de Thélusson; on July 27, 1781, two days after the sale had begun, Vitet spent 600 *livres* there.[18] Because no details are known about the pieces he bought, they cannot be traced in the inventories of either Madame de Thélusson or the duchess. On December 3 of the same year, the duchess asked Vitet to acquire other items at the sale held after the premature death of Mademoiselle Cécile Dumégnil, one of the most brilliant actresses of the day. Dumégnil lived in a *hôtel* on rue Bergère that had been luxuriously furnished a short while before by the *marchand-mercier* François-Charles Darnault and the *tapissier* Philippe-Bernard Allen.[19] Vitet's purchase amounted to 2,400 *livres*, but once again, since the pieces were not itemized, they cannot be traced in the inventories. We do know that Vitet bought two *bergères*, a night table, a chamber pot, and a basin with its ewer at the estate sale of the princesse de Rohan, which took place during the same period. The *bergères* are the sole pair described in the inventory: covered in blue satin embroidered with white silk, and placed in the ground-floor bedchamber of another *hôtel* on the place Royale.[20] After being reupholstered under Vitet's direction, they may have been used in the salon of either the duchess or the duke—the only two rooms in the Hôtel de La Trémoille in which a pair of *bergères* was inventoried.

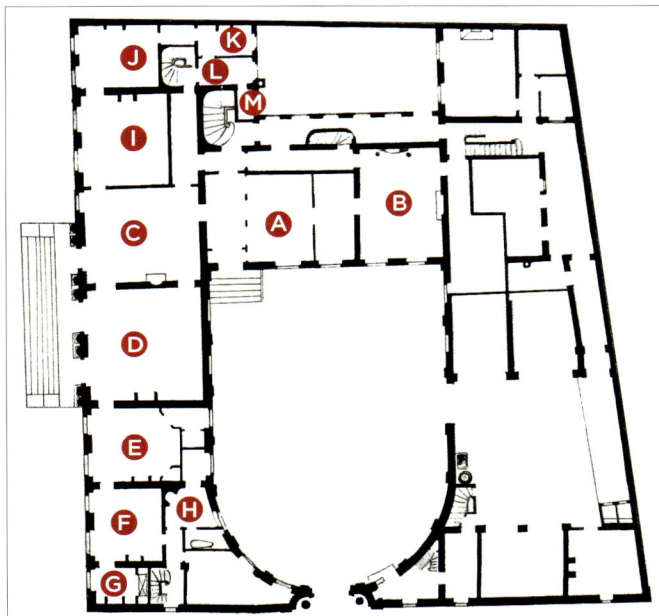

FIG. 35. Detail of fig. 32. Floor plan of the Hôtel de La Trémoille. Letters indicate the rooms described in the following text.

THE *APPARTEMENT DE SOCIÉTÉ*

The First Antechamber A

This room (see fig. 36) had a sober and functional decor, with neither mirrors nor curtains, and was plainly lit by a brass lantern with five panes of white glass. The seats, some of them refurbished, were simple, covered in sturdy woolen textiles suitable for withstanding the use of arriving guests: one bench seat was covered in tapestry and another in red velvet; nine old chairs in crimson Utrecht velvet; and six chairs in needlepoint. There was also a large pine table, something not usually found in an antechamber. Apart from a large sideboard with five doors, the room's remaining pieces were furniture in the form of an oak commode, another bench seat covered in tapestry, and a small cabinet that was painted gray, which in fact concealed the valets' beds.[21]

The Dining Room B

This room was lit by a large glass lantern and a second smaller one, both set in *tole* (tin). Like the antechamber, the dining room did not have curtains, but its two mirrors indicate a progression in the quality of the decor. One, a square mirror, was placed on the *trumeau* (pier) between the windows along the courtyard, and the other was in an arched niche on the opposite wall. In addition, the room was embellished with two plaster statues and a basin used for hand washing. Vitet bought most of the furniture in January 1783. The mahogany dessert table, with three compartments fitted with marble shelves, was purchased for 120 *livres*. The twenty-six painted wood chairs (ten armchairs *en cabriolet* and sixteen side chairs), covered in blue Utrecht velvet printed with white motifs, totaled 857 *livres* and 15 *sols*. They were accompanied by six chairs with woven rush seats costing 16 *livres* and 10 *sols*.[22] For the windows, Vitet had two pairs of curtains made, in blue and white taffeta edged with blue trim, as well as two small fine linen curtains edged with fine-thread ribbon, all for 294 *livres* and 6 *sols*. A few other pieces were also inventoried in the room: the round table with a pine top and an oak base, a small bench covered in crimson Utrecht velvet, a servant's cot, and a double ladder. Clearly demonstrating the progression of the decor and value of the furnishings relative to those of the antechamber, the dining room furniture was much more costly. Estimated at only 168 *livres* in 1790, it in fact had cost more than 1,300 *livres* seven years before.

The Second Antechamber, or Salle du Dais *(Audience Chamber)*

This room served both as antechamber for the *valets de chambre* and as *salle du dais*, where the duke could hold audiences. However, by the end of the eighteenth century, such use of the *salle du dais*, evoking the distant customs of Louis XIV, was becoming rare in Parisian ducal residences.[23] Often it was merely an antechamber in which various furnishings were stored at random. Such was the case at the Hôtel de La Trémoille.

The room's paneling was painted gray, and the walls displayed one large three-piece mirror. It was the only room in the *grands appartements* with a hanging, made of newly fashionable wallpaper, which imitated crimson damask. This color, highly conventional and very much expected for this type of room, was echoed in the two pairs of taffeta curtains edged with trim and in the velvet canopy, made of silk and white satin and trimmed in imitation gold, which Vitet bought for 516 *livres* on March 18, 1782. He had it embroidered with the duke's coat of arms for 96 *livres*. On March 26, he spent a little more than 400 *livres* to reupholster six armchairs and sixteen side chairs of gray-painted wood, covered in superfine crimson Utrecht velvet. In 1790, these chairs were inventoried in the neighboring Salon and estimated at only 150 *livres* (see Martin Chapman's history essay in this volume). This stately furnishing composed a setting that celebrated the dynastic renown of the house of La Trémoille: the walls were hung with five family portraits as well as two large paintings depicting the estates of Attichy and Thouars. Yet the formal layout was counterbalanced by a jumble of various small pieces of furniture for everyday use.

Stored here to free up space in the neighboring Salon were a small portable trictrac board in the form of a book and seven gaming tables, one made of mahogany and delivered by the cabinetmaker Nicolas Héricourt in spring 1782.[24] There was also a corner cupboard and a small wood-veneer cabinet, two fountains, a walnut night stand, and a servant's cot. Two paper-covered screens concealed these disparate items. Altogether, the objects in the room were valued at 630 *livres* during the inventory, a sum that clearly attests to an evolution in the quality of the decor relative to that of the preceding rooms.

THE DUCHESS'S *APPARTEMENT*

The Salon

The *appartements*' progressive enhancement of decor culminated in the Salon, the room where guests were received, situated both physically and socially at the center of the Hôtel de La Trémoille. Its function was closely linked to that of the bedchamber that followed it, as was its refurbishment, ordered by the duke even before he took possession of the property.

On June 24, 25, and 26, 1781, the joiner Demazeau removed the wainscoting and the parquet along with part of the bedroom paneling. One wall in the former configuration of the room, described in the inventory of August 1780, can be seen in a plate published by Blondel (see fig. 34).[25] Perpendicular to the window wall were two doors leading to the neighboring rooms, both surmounted by a painting depicting a subject from Aesop's fables in a carved giltwood frame with ornaments above. The same type of frame is also found around the mirrors in the *trumeaux* between the windows and

FIG. 36. Jean-Michel Chevotet (French, 1698–1772), cross section of the first antechamber, with its original paneling, of the Hôtel Béthune (later the Hôtel de Châtillon and the Hôtel de La Trémoille). Drawing for the etching in Jacques-François Blondel, *L'Architecture françoise* (Paris, 1752–1756). École nationale supérieure des Beaux-Arts, Paris. This drawing has been reversed for the purposes of engraving. Here the drawing, shown in reverse, depicts the correct orientation.

above the fireplace, the latter mirror flanked by carved panels. The wall opposite the windows and each adjacent wall were covered in fabric. The 1762 inventory following the death of the princesse de Tarente's father mentions a crimson damask wall covering measuring "vingt-six lés sur trois aunes de haut."[26] Delapoize doubtless considered these wall hangings too old-fashioned and replaced them with wood paneling with a more Neoclassical aspect; the symmetry of the doors and false doors, along with the mirrored *trumeaux* in the middle of each wall, offered a more definite architectural rhythm. Sculpted bas-reliefs replaced the decorative paintings above the doors as well. The final effect better reflected the sense of propriety suitable for a reception room within a ducal residence (see fig. 37 for comparison).

The Salon was the first room in the *appartement* in which the wood paneling, besides being painted gray and carved, was lavishly gilded. Two French windows in the room opened out to the steps leading down to the garden. Four large mirrors, newly installed, amply reflected daylight. This room had the greatest number of mirrors in the *hôtel*, an obvious sign of opulence. The artificial lighting was equally abundant. Each of the three *trumeaux* was framed by a pair of three-branch gilt-bronze wall lights (in the other rooms, the sconces had only two branches).

A twelve-branch white crystal chandelier hung from the center of the ceiling. Finally, two small crystal girandoles mounted in gilt bronze on bases painted to imitate lacquer were placed on the chimneypiece. Shielded by a white metal screen of six panels, the hearth was furnished with a set of large polished iron firedogs surmounted by a vase

FIG. 37. Johann Christian Kammsetzer (German, active Poland, 1753–1795), *Elevation of the Salon of the Hôtel Grimod de la Reynière*, 1782. Brown ink, watercolor, and traces of graphite, gouache, and wash, 10⅞ × 17 in. (27.7 × 43.3 cm). The Print Room of the University of Warsaw Library, Warsaw.

of gilt bronze and their *surtout* (cover) in tin. Also on the mantel were a pair of jasper vases and three large lidded vases of blue and white porcelain with gilding. This array of ornaments—seven pieces in all—left little room for the most expensive clock in the house, estimated at 600 *livres*. Its movement, by Ledunois, counted the hours, minutes, and seconds, as well as days and months. Its case and its base were decorated in the form of a pilaster with figures and other ornaments of gilt bronze. The clock was more likely displayed on one of the two consoles topped with white marble. The other console showed two bouquets of artificial flowers in porcelain bowls covered in glass vitrines. Indeed, the clock was inventoried not with the chimneypiece ornaments but following the consoles and the sconces that appear to have gone with them. These consoles were the only furniture in the *appartement* to be precisely documented (see fig. 38). Sené's woodwork was carved by Royer *père* at a set price of 300 *livres* per piece. The gilder's report by Royer *fils* gives a complete description of the design:[27]

> The two console tables for the salon, gilded with burnished gold, the apron of which is ornamented with egg and dart, pearls strung in a double row, an openwork frieze of rosettes and husks in varying shapes and four great rosettes in the corners of the frame, the astragal carved in the form of myrtle, the middle of said frieze decorated with a wreath of flowers crowning a head of the sun set against the sun's rays, beneath which are two olive branches, tied with a ribbon; the two pilasters behind the scrolled consoles

adorned by a capital with foliage ornament and by seven flower heads in the fluting, two rosettes in the corners, and a husk below; the two scrolled consoles adorned with two rows of pearls on each side and on the back a double husk with isolated foliage ornament and on the front a curling acanthus leaf at the top and with parsley leaves coming from the same leaf, with a garland circling the three sides of the console and with two rosettes at the top and the bottom, supported by a husk-shaped foot, the stretcher adorned with tracery upon which rests a vase embellished with various ornaments and its handles likewise with leaves, and with three garlands, one of which is horseshoe-shaped, and the other two falling at the sides, the whole finely gilded, finely recut and with gold of the highest quality, estimated at 408 *livres* each, together they add up to 816 *livres*[28]

On July 27, 1781, when the work had just begun, Vitet bought furniture for both the Salon and the duchess's bedroom, paying 6,660 *livres* for all. The specific items and the names of the sellers are unknown, but in light of the 1790 inventory, the pieces were probably used in those rooms. However, the listing of three side chairs is

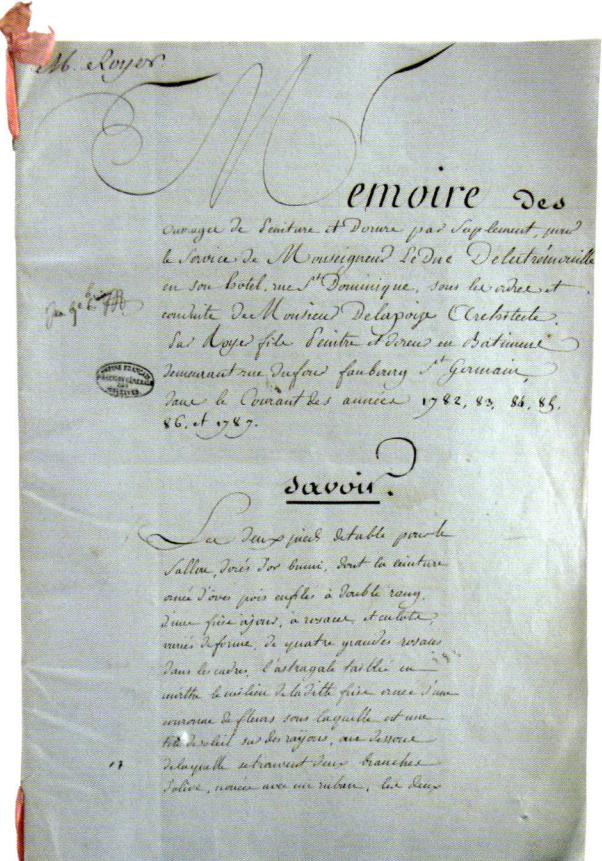

FIG. 38 (*above left*). Account from the Salon inventory of 1790, with reference to the gilding for the consoles, conducted between 1782 and 1787. Archives Nationales, Paris, MC/ET/LVII/597. FIG. 39 (*above right*). Antoine Vitet's account for the furnishings of the *hôtel*, ca. 1780s. Archives Nationales, Paris.

surprising, both because one would expect an even number of chairs and because the contemporary salons of dukes usually contained eight to twelve of them.

The rest of the furniture, however, perfectly followed the norms for seating found in ducal homes of the 1780s: twelve armchairs, two *bergères*, and one sofa provided with a seat cushion and two pillows. This giltwood ensemble was covered in blue and white damask, as was a small group of seats for everyday use consisting of seven small armchairs *en cabriolet*, four of which were provided with seat cushions, also of carved wood but simply painted gray. On March 26, 1782, Vitet bought blue and white checked taffeta to have dust covers made for these seats. Even though the use of damask was quite customary for such rooms, the colors were completely unusual for the residence of a duke. Among some forty inventories of salons studied for this period, blue never appears as the dominant color. The textiles for these rooms are most often crimson, if damask or velvet is used, or white if the material is embroidered, brocaded, painted cotton, or chiné taffeta. It is equally surprising to find curtains in the duchess's Salon that were made of the same fabric as the seats. Generally a plain silk fabric—gros de Tours, *quinze-seize*, or taffeta[29]—in a coordinating color was preferred for curtains. Likewise, the use of a valence at the window suggested more the exuberant tastes of bankers or stage actresses than the dignity and decorum of a duke. Also on March 26, 1782, Vitet bought some blue Utrecht velvet printed with white motifs to cover two *voyeuses* (low seated chairs with high backs for watching gaming). Two more would be covered in January 1783 with this same fabric, together with the dining room chairs. While seven gaming tables were stored in the neighboring *salle du dais*, the only cabinetwork pieces deliberately left in the Salon at the time of the 1790 inventory were "two mahogany breakfast tables with pedestal bases and a white marble top edged in gilt brass" and six small mahogany screens covered with blue taffeta.[30] Finally, it should be noted that the Salon had a single set of furniture that was used year round; there were no summer and winter furnishings, as in the homes of the ducs d'Aiguillon, d'Estrée, de Praslin, and de Richelieu. These two seasons were distinguished only by the addition of a carpet in winter.[31]

The Bedchamber

The duchess's bedchamber was the next most richly decorated and furnished room in the house. Its furniture was estimated at 1,900 *livres* in 1790, a bit more than that of the Salon, appraised at 1,654 *livres*. The duchess created two small spaces in front of each of the two windows overlooking the courtyard. In one of these spaces she had a bedroom put in for a chambermaid, in which a canopy bed of blue and white printed cotton and a walnut night table were inventoried. In the other a small wardrobe containing various furnishings for everyday use or for hygiene (a night table, two commode chairs in the form of armchairs, a bidet covered in red morocco leather, eight porcelain or earthenware chamber pots, an earthenware water pitcher and basin, two potpourri jars, and a night lamp of silver-plated copper). In front of the two additions was an alcove intended to hold a bed, replacing the mirrored *trumeau* found between the two windows in 1780.

With gray-painted wood paneling highlighted

in gold, the room was firmly inscribed within the continuity of the Salon Doré and the *appartement de société*. Indeed, its furnishing was conventional and "in good taste," with few personal touches or paintings. Besides four overdoors painted on canvas, which may have been retained from the previous decor, there were only three small family portraits painted on canvas and eight others in pastel to celebrate the dynasty. With solely the two windows on the garden side remaining, daylight was reflected by three mirrors with carved and gilded frames: one on the chimneypiece *trumeau*, flanked by a pair of two-branch sconces, the second one opposite, and the third between the windows. As in the Salon, the fireplace was provided with a six-panel screen and a set of polished iron firedogs, each decorated with three pinecones.[32] The mantel shelf doubtless held the clock mentioned in the inventory: signed "Cochon, Paris," placed in a case carried by two figures with ornaments, the whole in gilt bronze with a marble pedestal and a protective glass vitrine.

The main furniture consisted of a *lit à la turque* with ostrich feathers, two large *bergères*, plus four large armchairs and two small armchairs with seat cushions, all in carved and gilded wood. Four armchairs with seat cushions and two side chairs in gray-painted wood completed the furnishings. Estimated at 1,200 *livres* in the 1790 inventory,[33] the ensemble, in various woods, was unified by its fabric covering, a green and white damask also used for two pairs of curtains. These curtains, since they were inventoried without their rods, were evidently hung *à l'italienne*, that is, drawn up on strings. As in the Salon, the seat covers were in checked taffeta (here, green and white). Also as in the Salon, the carpet was removed for cleaning in autumn 1789. Although many of the pieces were of cabinetwork, they had to be rather old, given the low value of all of them (240 *livres* in 1790). Most of the pieces were made of inlaid wood with gilt-bronze ornaments: a commode with two large and three small drawers, its top made of breccia marble;[34] a little two-drawer *chiffonière* with a marble top; a one-drawer *sauteuse* (small commode), also with a marble top; a small table with four legs; and a diminutive secretary with compartments. Two rosewood corner cabinets were evidently of older design, since rosewood was no longer much used in the 1780s. In contrast, the presence of a few mahogany pieces was a sign of modernity. Mahogany was used for a small table with three compartments and a console with two compartments and a marble top, which was more fashionable than the usual type with carved and gilded wood. This console replaced an earlier one made of bloodwood that Vitet bought for 180 *livres* in March 1782. Several small furnishings completed the ensemble: four small screens covered in green taffeta;[35] a small caned stool closed on the sides so that it could hold papers; a side chair with a woven rush seat; and a dog bed with a green damask cushion.

The Library 🅕

Here and in the rest of the duchess's suite, the formality of the furnishing of the previous rooms was abandoned in favor of a personal atmosphere. As in the Salon, the duchess had the wall covering removed and replaced by gray-painted wood paneling and two false doors. Above both the false and the actual doors were four oval paintings on canvas; their subject is not recorded. The frames of the mirrored fireplace *trumeau* and the *trumeau* between the windows, also painted gray, were probably retained from the previous state.³⁶ The paneling clearly lacked any gilding.

Bookcases were set up around the room. On March 26, 1782, Vitet had nine curtains of yellow and white checked taffeta hung on the doors, matching the room's furnishing. The same day, he purchased, for 105 *livres*, fire grates of polished iron adorned with gilt-bronze vases for the fireplace. The mantel received two porcelain vases with their stoppers and a *magot de la Chine* (Chinese figure) in porcelain. The room was lit not by the usual sconces but by a small lantern with five panes of white glass mounted in gilt bronze and by two crystal girandoles. A small, wall-hung clock in a gilt-bronze case, signed "Fassé à l'observatoire," told the time. The room's furniture, covered in satin brocade with white and yellow background, consisted of four armchairs (covered in yellow and white taffeta) and four side chairs, matched by two pairs of window curtains in the same yellow and white checked taffeta. A large winged armchair with a green damask cushion and four chairs with woven rush seats and lyre backs completed the ensemble. As in the Salon and the bedroom, a carpet covered the floor during the winter. The library contained numerous pieces of cabinetwork: a large three-drawer *bureau* of inlaid wood with a top of black morocco leather, adorned with two column-shaped candlesticks in gilt white porcelain and a small inkwell of a similar fashion; a fall-front secretary of inlaid wood with gilt-bronze mounts and a marble top;³⁷ a small *chiffonière* in wood veneer and gilt bronze; a little bookshelf; a small rosewood strongbox on a base of the same wood; a rosewood table with a lead basin and its lid; a small *coffre de toilette* (dressing case); a walnut *sauteuse*; an oak library ladder with six rungs; and two small green taffeta screens.³⁸ Including a painted *tole* teapot provided with silver-plated copper, the whole set of furnishings was appraised at 598 *livres*.

The Boudoir

The series of rooms along the garden ended with a small room whose window opened onto the garden. In 1780 this room, lacking a fireplace and mirror, served as an *arrière-cabinet* (closet). Here the duchess set up a small boudoir. Its gray-painted paneling, highlighted in gold, was embellished with painted flowers and four mirrored pilasters. A fireplace was installed, above which a mirrored *trumeau* was flanked by a pair of two-branch gilt-bronze wall sconces. In the hearth, polished iron firedogs were adorned by gilt-bronze pinecones, and, on the mantel, two ornaments were each supported by three little putti. In place of the wall cupboard that faced the window in 1780, a niche was created with a draped ottoman daybed, hung with draperies and provided with a cushion and two pillows. This sofa and four giltwood side chairs were covered using two pieces of satin on a gray background with a motif of brocaded bouquets.³⁹ It is not possible, however, to tell whether the white taffeta that Vitet bought for the window curtains was used as the main material or for the lining. On January 21, 1783, Vitet completed the furnishing for this room with his purchase of a *bergère* covered in green and white checked taffeta. Numerous dishes were also inventoried: an *écuelle* (broth bowl or porringer) with its plate and lid in porcelain with gilt outlines; a teapot and its lid placed on a dish warmer, all in porcelain; two coffee sets, one with sixteen and the other with seventeen different porcelain pieces; six coffee cups with their saucers and lids in blue and white porcelain set on a lacquered tray; and two breakfast services in porcelain and a third in *terre anglaise* (creamware) on their varnished tin trays. This welter of small precious objects was completed by a bouquet of artificial flowers in biscuit porcelain kept under a glass vitrine, twelve porcelain flower vases, four blue glass vases mounted in gilt copper, two carps, and several damaged or broken figures in different types of porcelain. Perhaps some of the pieces intended for the library had been placed in the boudoir at the time of the inventory.

The Dressing Room H

The duchess's *appartement* ended with a small dressing room set up behind the curve of the great courtyard. The room, illuminated by a window, was covered in gray-painted paneling on which four family portraits were hung, along with fourteen small prints under glass and two little devotional paintings, all in their giltwood frames. It was heated by a fireplace, furnished with a set of polished iron firedogs with silver-plated ornaments. Above the fireplace, a mirrored *trumeau* framed in giltwood reflected two figures in biscuit under a glass vitrine and a clock of white marble and gilt bronze. A printed cotton with small bouquets painted on a white background covered two armchairs and two side chairs painted gray and protected by dust covers in checked fabric. For the one window, Vitet bought on March 26, 1782, a pair of white curtains edged in painted fabric. At her dressing table, the duchess had a cane armchair with a cushion of red morocco leather; the simple table, in white wood with an oak base, must have been covered with a fabric that was inventoried with the family's lace. The only cabinetwork in the room was a *chiffonière* of inlaid wood with a marble top adorned with gilt bronzes and a cherrywood corner cabinet. It is surprising not to find in this room any domestic objects besides a handled cup and its white glass saucer.

THE DUKE'S *APPARTEMENT*

Crossing back through the Salon and the *salle du dais*, the visitor would come to the duke's *appartement*. It consisted of a bedroom and a small salon, each with two windows overlooking the garden, as well as a study illuminated by a window that looked out on the kitchen courtyard. The layout is thus more basic than that of the duchess's *appartement*, with the duke's only room for retreat being his study. Furnished mostly in late 1782 and early 1783, the *appartement* also evinced more sober tastes: the rooms were simply painted gray, with no mention of the gilding (even on the chairs) that one would expect in a duke's *appartement*.

The Bedroom I

The bedroom was heated by a fireplace that was furnished with a set of polished iron firedogs decorated with gilt-bronze pinecones and, as in the Salon and the duchess's bedroom, a small, six-panel white metal screen. A pair of two-branch gilt-bronze sconces flanked the arched mirrored *trumeau* above the fireplace. Four overdoors painted on canvas depicted birds. The room's furnishing fabric was silk, in a lampas known as three-color damask, with a crimson background, estimated at 800 *livres* at the time of the inventory. It was used for a *lit à la turque* adorned with three panaches of feathers, two pairs of curtains, four armchairs, and three *bergères*. A few pieces of cabinetwork completed the ensemble. The commode of inlaid wood—a piece found in almost every eighteenth-century bedroom—had five drawers, with gilt-bronze ornaments and a white marble top. There was also a small breakfast table of similar material and a *bonheur du jour* described as "a little secretary of inlaid wood with a *serre papier* [filing cabinet] with sliding sides." It was accompanied by a desk chair in crimson morocco leather and two small mahogany screens covered in green taffeta—colors and fabric that were usual for this type of furnishing, although differing from the other fabrics in the room. Along with six small pastel paintings and the fireplace furniture, these various pieces were estimated at the meager sum of 140 *livres*.

The Salon

Concluding the enfilade along the garden, the next room was called the salon in the inventory, a denomination that was a sign of the times. One or two decades earlier, the room would no doubt have been called a *cabinet de compagnie* or simply a *cabinet*. It was the most richly furnished room of the duke's *appartement*. The furniture was estimated at some thirty *livres* less than that of the bedroom, but the latter was almost twice as large. The room's modest size seemed more expansive thanks to a play of mirrored *trumeaux*: one above the fireplace, a second on the facing wall, and a third between the windows. Only the fireplace *trumeau* received a pair of two-branch sconces. An eight-branch chandelier in gilt bronze, hung from a cord embellished by two tassels, completed the lighting. The hearth was furnished with a set of polished iron firedogs adorned with gilt-bronze pinecones, similar to that in the bedroom but smaller.⁴⁰

The chimneypiece was furthermore decorated with four small vases, two of porcelain with flowers and gilt outlines and two of *terre d'Angleterre*, as well as a bouquet of artificial flowers beneath a glass vitrine. The clock, by Charles Le Roy, was set in a gilt-bronze cartel (wall-hung) case. The salon's silk furnishings, purchased in March 1782, consisted of a pair of curtains, two sofas, ten armchairs, and two *bergères*. Vitet re-covered them in yellow lampas with a white motif, purchased at 1,610 *livres* for 70 ells.⁴¹ Reserved for formal use, this movable furniture was protected by red and white checked covers; it is unknown whether the pieces were painted or gilded. The ensemble was completed by six armchairs and six side chairs intended for everyday use; they were covered in yellow Utrecht velvet, and their wood was simply painted gray. With its twenty-six seats, this room seems quite cluttered, the more so because it also contained a mahogany fortepiano, the fashionable instrument of the day, which dethroned the harpsichord at the end of the eighteenth century. In contrast, the room had few pieces of cabinetwork: only a lacquer chest with carved giltwood feet and two corner cabinets of inlaid wood with an étagère above. They presumably displayed a second bouquet of artificial flowers with three stuffed birds beneath a glass vitrine, a large porcelain service of some thirty pieces, and a small tin fountain with feet, handles, and faucet in silver-plated copper. In addition to two overdoors painted on canvas, whose subjects are unknown, the salon was hung with nine family portraits, also painted on canvas.

The Study

Behind the duke's salon lay his study. This small room, with an *entresol* above, was heated by a *cheminée à la prussienne*, a sort of small stove placed in the fireplace, the open hearth provided with the same set of firedogs as those in the bedroom and the salon. Standing on the mantel, in front of the mirrored *trumeau*, was a little clock in its case, decorated in gilt bronze, on a white marble pedestal. The only lighting in the room was provided by a silver-plated night lamp; a gilt-bronze lamp protected by white glass; and two small figures in biscuit porcelain, each supporting a bobeche to hold a candle. The furnishings, in blue and white lampas, were kept to a minimum: one pair of curtains, two side chairs, and two armchairs painted gray. There were also two lyre-back chairs with woven rush seats and a winged armchair in Utrecht velvet with a blue and white mosaic print. Two bookcases hung with blue taffeta curtains were integrated in the paneling. The duke did his work on a cylinder desk in inlaid wood provided with gilt bronzes. He also had a small walnut writing desk. Several other objects completed the room's furnishing: a *table en badine* with a steel hook, a walnut night table, two little flower vases in blue-painted earthenware, a small water pitcher in white glass, and two diminutive urns in blue glass.

The Valet's Bedroom

Also looking out on the kitchen courtyard, the *valet de chambre*'s bedroom was heated by a small earthenware stove. In addition to a small bed with a canopy of blue and white chiné hangings, it contained several household or hygiene items: a walnut bidet covered in red morocco leather with a white earthenware basin and a pewter syringe, a water pitcher and its basin (also of white earthenware), a small brass candlestick, and, in an armoire, a copper warming pan to heat the duke's bed and a second walnut bidet with its earthenware basin and pewter syringe.

The Lieux à l'Anglaise

Another service area, situated at the far end of this small room, the *lieux à l'anglaise* (water closet) likewise looked out on the kitchen courtyard. Inventoried there were a third walnut bidet, a bidet chair provided with red morocco leather, and two earthenware chamber pots.

CONCLUSION

Almost entirely redecorated and refurnished between 1781 and 1783, the *grands appartements* of the Hôtel de La Trémoille on rue Saint-Dominique were very much conventional: the types of gilding, fabrics, and furniture all followed the conventions of good taste befitting the social rank of a duke. The gradual enhancement of the decor from one room to the next is clearly evident not only in the progression of light sources and mirrors, but also in the use of gilding and fabrics.

It is nonetheless possible to discern certain unique aspects of the duke and duchess's aesthetic choices. There is a noticeable lack of folding screens (except in the second antechamber), which were inevitable elements of eighteenth-century Parisian interiors. More importantly, the colorful range of fabrics merits a closer look. Crimson clearly prevailed in Enlightenment interiors, especially those of high-ranking figures such as kings, princes, and dukes; here it is found only in the solemn *salle du dais* and in the duke's bedroom. White, the second most frequently used color in the period, is used here solely in the duchess's dressing room. However, the repeated use of blue in three rooms (the dining room, the grand Salon, and the duke's study) seems distinctive to the Hôtel de La Trémoille, as does the use of yellow (in the duchess's library and the duke's salon), which is rarely found in other residences. Finally, the choice of gray, in the duchess's boudoir, likewise denotes exceptional originality. In terms of the curtains, those at the La Trémoille residence were rarely made of a solid fabric (gros de Tours, *quinze-seize*, or taffeta), as was normally the case in France since the end of the seventeenth century. Here, too, the La Trémoilles upheld this convention only in the *salle du dais*. Although they did use taffeta for the dining room curtains and for those of the duchess's library, they rather imaginatively chose checked taffeta (blue and white for the former, yellow and white for the latter). Most surprising was the systematic use of lampas, a relatively costly fabric, for the curtains in rooms in which the furniture was also covered in lampas.

Exploiting the richness and variety of archival sources has allowed us to evoke the interior of the La Trémoille residence, which has never before been known. This study, undertaken on the occasion of the restoration of the paneling and furniture of the *hôtel*'s Salon, aims to produce a coherent picture that might convey the atmosphere of the original house.

NOTES

1 The archival documents are cited in *Le faubourg Saint-Germain: La rue Saint-Dominique: Hôtels et amateurs* (Paris, 1984). The inventory was discovered in December 2012.
2 Archives Nationales (hereafter AN), Paris, Z/1j/1068.
3 AN, T//1051/46, *cote* 526, and T//1051/48, *cote* 539.
4 The family's earlier *hôtel* still exists today at 62 rue du Temple in Paris. I thank Alexandre Gady for this information.
5 Michel Gallet, *Les architectes parisiens du XVIIIe siècle* (Paris, 1995), 268–69.
6 AN, T//1051/61.
7 Jacques-François Blondel, *L'Architecture françoise . . . Paris, 1752–1756* (Paris, 1904), 1:249.
8 Ibid., 1:218.
9 AN, T//1051/1 and Z/1j/1064, August 16, 1780.
10 AN, Z//1j/1168.
11 AN, Z//1j/1167.
12 AN, T//1051/55.
13 AN, T//1051/61, *cote* 701.
14 AN, T//1051/48, *cote* 539, *pièce* 173.
15 Ibid., *cote* 553, *pièce* 219.
16 AN, T//1051/49, *cote* 553, *pièce* 659.
17 AN, T//1051/48, *cote* 540, *pièce* 351, and T//1051/49, *cote* 554, *pièce* 176.
18 AN, T//1051/46, *cote* 526, *pièce* 265; MC/ET/LXXII/1021, inventory of July 7, 1781; *Annonces, affiches et avis divers*, no. 202, July 27, 1781, 1719. Madame de Thélusson then lived in a house on the corner of boulevard and rue d'Artois, rented from the *fermier-général* (royal tax collector) Grimod de La Reynière, not in the *hôtel* that she just had built by Ledoux on rue de la Chaussée d'Antin.
19 AN, T//1051/46, *cote* 526, *pièce* 412; Y//11507, *scellés* of August 19, 1781; MC/ET/CIX/761, inventory of August 29, 1781; *Annonces, affiches et avis divers*, no. 330, November 26, 1781, 2723.
20 Today the place des Vosges.
21 The estimated value of these few pieces, along with a double ladder, was a mere 66 *livres*.
22 Only three of them were inventoried in 1790.
23 Although the tradition was still upheld in the *appartements* of the duc de Rohan-Rohan (prince de Soubise) as well as those of the duc de Fitz-James and in the homes of the old duc de Richelieu, marshal of France, and the duchesse de Mazarin, a great many others, such as the Aumont, Brissac, and Clermont-Tonnerre families, had abandoned it. In some *hôtels*

24. AN, T//1051/48, *cote* 539, *pièce* 173.
25. Blondel, *L'Architecture françoise*, Hôtel de Béthune, no. 17, plate 3.
26. "26 fabric widths by 3 ells high." AN, MC/ET/CXII/578, December 1, 1762. Inventory upon the death of the duc de Châtillon, no. 189.
27. AN, T//1051/55, *cote* 605.
28. The price was reduced to 750 *livres* by Delapoize.
29. Gros de Tours, *quinze-seize*, and taffeta are all plain silk fabrics of different lengths.
30. Purchased by Vitet for 6 *livres* apiece on December 4, 1782.
31. Vitet bought the carpet for 792 *livres* on February 20, 1782. Because it had been sent to the master upholsterer Jean Bellat for restoration on November 10, 1789, it was not inventoried after the duchess's death.
32. Acquired by Vitet on July 27, 1781, for 182 *livres* and 13 *sols*.
33. When cited below in the text, "the inventory" refers to that of 1790.
34. Purchased by Vitet for 179 *livres* in March 1782.
35. For which Vitet paid 30 *livres* on December 4, 1782.
36. Their dimensions are identical in the report of 1780 and the inventory of 1790.
37. Which Vitet bought for 84 *livres* in March 1782.
38. Purchased by Vitet for 9 *livres* on December 4, 1782.
39. This fabric was purchased by Vitet for 312 *livres* in 1782.
40. Purchased by Vitet for 108 *livres* on December 4, 1782.
41. 90.3 yards (82.6 meters).

the room was retained without its formal function; for instance, it became a dining room in the home of the dowager duchesse de Luynes.

APPENDIX: SERVANTS TO THE HOUSE OF LA TRÉMOILLE

This list itemizes the 42 servants working for the La Trémoille family in the beginning of the 1780s, many of whom would have worked at the Hôtel de La Trémoille in Paris. The French is taken verbatim from the original documents found in the Archives Nationales, Paris.

1. Pierre. *Intendant* (steward)
2. Mesnil, Gabriel Jacques. *Intendant* (steward)
3. Reymond. *Maître d'hôtel* (butler)
4. Palluel, François. *Garçon de cuisine* (cook)
5. Bidault. *Aide de cuisine* (assistant cook)
6. Guerhard. *Officier d'office* (head of the butler's pantry)
7. Hubert. *Gardien* (guard, Hôtel Saint-Avoye, then de Châtillon)
8. Vomberg. *Concierge* (caretaker, Versailles *hôtel*)
9. Pithon. *Suisse* (porter or gatekeeper)
10. Guérin. *Pourvoyeur* (purveyor for supplies)
11. Lafrance. *Valet de pied* (footman)
12. Maraine. *Valet de pied* (footman)
13. Lonchamp. *Valet de pied* (footman for the duchess)
14. Ramard, Jean-Jacques. *Valet de pied* (footman for the duchess)
15. Verner, Jean. *Valet de pied* (footman)
16. Castel, Antoine Cabal. *Valet de chambre* (manservant)
17. Demont, Jacques-Louis. *Valet de chambre* (manservant)
18. Vitet, Antoine. *Valet de chambre* (manservant, upholsterer for the duchess)
19. Heussée. *Valet de chambre* (manservant, upholsterer for the duke)
20. Hector. *Nègre* (African page for the duke)
21. Francy. *Femme de charge* (housekeeper)
22. Demont. *Femme de chambre* (housemaid)
23. Julie. *Femme de chambre* (housemaid)
24. Payen. *Fille de garde-robe* (wardrobe maid for the duchess)
25. Velay de Lajeunesse, Joseph Viard. *Froteur* (cleaner)
26. Vellay, Antoine. *Froteur* (cleaner)
27. Tiron. *Écuyer* (horseman or equerry)
28. Lefèvre. *Cocher* (coachman for the duke)
29. Potel. *Cocher* (coachman)
30. Cadet. *Postillon* (postilion or messenger)
31. François. *Postillon* (postilion or messenger)
32. Charpentier. *Piqueur* (stud groom)
33. Lajeunesse. *Palfrenier* (groom)
34. Leveillé. *Palfrenier* (groom)
35. Malenfant. *Palfrenier* (groom)
36. Serail, Jean. *Palfrenier* (groom)
37. Veber. *Chasseur* (page)
38. Sollet. *Jardinier* (gardener)
39. Heitz. *Gouverneur* (princes' tutor)
40. Perrin. *Précepteur de princes* (princes' tutor)
41. Dupont. *Valet de pied* (footman for the prince de Tarente)
42. Miller. *Valet de chambre* (manservant for the princes)

A NOTE ON THE UPHOLSTERY

Xavier Bonnet

In the absence of physical evidence or archival sources, restoration of upholstery can be a perilous undertaking. The artisanal practices of today's upholsterers must be qualified by a historical approach that can justify the aesthetic choices made.

To this day, none of the pieces of furniture from the Salon from the Hôtel de La Trémoille has been identified. The discovery of the 1790 inventory of the room, at a time when restoration work and the acquisition of furniture had already begun, has enabled us to specify the nature and color of the fabrics, the types of window embellishment, and the numbers and types of seats as well as the finishes of their wood frames and the style of their covering. However, several questions remained unanswered, making it necessary to specify numerous details on the basis of reliable historical sources. Thus, to the extent possible, each of these choices has been informed by a document or archive from the 1780s (see fig. 40, for example).

FIG. 40. Section through the Grand Salon of the Hôtel de Salm, ca. 1780s. Pen and ink and watercolor. Musée national de la Légion d'honneur et des ordres de la chevalerie, Paris. This image shows the use of blue fabric in the home of the duchesse de La Trémoille's brother, the prince de Salm.

CHOICE OF MATERIALS

Fabrics

In light of eighteenth-century practices, the "blue and white damask" mentioned in the 1790 inventory of the Salon would refer to lampas with a blue background and a white motif. Several fabrics of this kind can be found today in the collections or archives of silk manufacturers in Lyon, although it is difficult to prove the absolute authenticity of the design. Indeed, often in the nineteenth century the furnishing silks were rewoven, modifying the patterns or the play of weave and color to produce a fabric sometimes quite distant from the original eighteenth-century model. The 1790 inventory says nothing of the fabric patterns.

The lampas (a damask-like silk) that we have chosen from the archives of Tassinari & Chatel in Lyon, successors of the famed Camille Pernon and Grand Frères, is of two self-patterned wefts, with an arabesque design characteristic of the 1780s (see figs. 41, 42). Comparison of Tassinari's lampas with a curtain conserved at the Mobilier National in Paris, made of the same fabric and bearing an inventory mark from the early nineteenth century,[1] and with an incomplete piece conserved at the Musée Historique des Tissus in Lyon[2] revealed that what we first thought to be an authentic eighteenth-century textile was in fact a nineteenth-century reweaving. Thus, the re-worked design was established based on the archive of the Musée Historique des Tissus (see fig. 43), which enabled us to restore the original details and the weaves. However, since the background color of this fragment was light green, the coloration was changed to be compatible with the mention in the 1790 inventory (see fig. 44). Here

FIG. 41 (*facing left*). Full-length *mise en carte* (textile design) by Tassinari & Chatel, 2013.

FIG. 42 (*facing right*). Full-length silk textile by Tassinari & Chatel, 2013.

FIG. 43 (*above*). Xavier Bonnet at the Musée Historique des Tissus, Lyon, with the eighteenth-century document and a later reweaving by Tassinari & Chatel, probably nineteenth century.

FIG. 44 (*right*). Furnishing silk, Lyon, ca. 1790. Musée Historique des Tissus, Lyon, MT 27893.2. This silk was used as a document for the color of the new reweaving for the Salon.

another item from the Musée Historique des Tissus served as a reference: a brocaded lampas, two self-patterned wefts,[3] that clearly had no long-term exposure to sunlight, because its colors are exceptionally well preserved.

Trimmings

Although the inventory of 1790 offers information about the fabrics, it gives no indication of the trimmings. Other examples from the same period, however—whether pictorial sources, surviving works, or the registers of upholsterers such as Claude-François Capin or Charles Delarue—provide some of the answers. From these we know that the drapery and curtains were edged with a gimp and embellished with fringes and tassels, and that the finishing for seats covered in lampas was generally done with gimp rather than gilt nails.

The trimmings for the curtains and drapery are modeled on those of a canopy bed conserved at the Hôtel de Berny in Amiens (fig. 45).[4] The red and white colors of the original were changed to blue and white (see fig. 46). The fringe along the edges of the drapery and curtains is embellished with alternating *torsades* and *jasmins* spaced about 2.7 cm apart. The heights of the reference models (5.4 cm and 6.07 cm) were increased to balance the proportions with the window height. The fringe used for the drapery measures 8.1 cm, while the one along the bottom of the curtains is 5.4 cm. The gimp that accompanies the fringe and trims the sides of the curtains and drapery is a *crête giroline* (loop gimp) made up of three guipures (cords used for trimming), 2.7 cm high. The model for the tassels that hold the drapery was copied in its entirety.

The trimming placed on the chairs is a *crête à clouer* (gimp) made up of three guipures, measuring ten *lignes* (2.25 cm). It adopts a classical model from the late eighteenth century, found notably on a set of armchairs covered in lampas in a private collection near Tours. The edges of the sofa cushion and those of the *bergères* were embellished by a *corde à puits* likewise based on a classical model from the end of the eighteenth century. It can be seen, for example, on a *bergère* cushion from the gallery of the Château de Chanteloup, conserved at the J. Paul Getty Museum, Los Angeles.[5]

FIG. 45 (*above left*). Detail of textile and *passementerie* (trim) design from the Hôtel de Berny in Amiens, ca. 1770.

FIG. 46 (*above right*). Detail of contemporary silk reweaving by Tassinari & Chatel, with *passementerie* by Declercq, made for the Salon, 2013.

FIG. 47. Design for a curtain, 1775–1800. Pen and black ink, brush and watercolor, and graphite on off-white laid paper, 9 7/16 × 7 1/8 in. (23.9 × 18.1 cm). Cooper-Hewitt, National Design Museum, New York, purchased for the Museum by the Advisory Council, 1908-26-137.

FABRICATION OF THE FURNISHINGS

Window Embellishments

The model for the window embellishments comes from a design at the Cooper-Hewitt, National Design Museum (fig. 47), which was implemented by comparing the design to the bed drapery at the Hôtel de Berny and to Capin's supply register for the Crown's *garde-meuble* (furniture repository). The valence consists of a drapery of two festoons, bordered at both sides by a tail (see fig. 48). The drapery and tails are lined with linen cloth and, on the lower part, with color-coordinated taffeta. The bottom of the elements is edged with a long fringe. The *crête giroline* was then applied at the head of the fringe by turning the loops toward the interior of the piece, and at the top of the tails by turning the loops toward the exterior.

The curtains, hung from underneath the

FIG. 48. Rendering of the curtain design for the Salon Doré by Atelier Saint-Louis.

valence, are made of unlined lampas. The widths of fabric were assembled with a flat felled seam described by Bimont[6] and illustrated in Diderot and d'Alembert's encyclopedia.[7] The bottom is decorated with a fringe and the edges are embellished with gimp, in the same fashion as the drapery tails.

Padding Styles

The 1790 inventory does not mention seat cushions on the *chaises courantes*, which means that they had a fixed upholstery and no cushion. The thriftiness that governed the furnishing of the *hôtel* on rue Saint-Dominique at the beginning of the 1780s would imply that the duke probably did not order *à l'anglaise* padding. This type of padding, which gave the horsehair stuffing a square shape, first appeared in France in the late 1760s and was still rare in Paris around 1780. At that time it seems to have been considered a refinement reserved for certain luxurious seats (see fig. 49). Thus, we did not adopt this technique in restoring the side chairs and armchairs for the Salon from the Hôtel de La Trémoille. Instead, they were restuffed *à l'ordinaire*, using the method described by Bimont and illustrated in Diderot and d'Alembert's encyclopedia. It produces very

A Note on the Upholstery

FIG. 49. Attributed to César van Loo (French, 1743–1821), *The Marquis d'Ossun*, ca. 1780. Oil on canvas, 85 13/16 × 64 5/8 in. (218 × 164.1 cm). National Gallery of Art, Washington, DC, gift of Mrs. Albert J. Beveridge in memory of her grandfather, Franklin Spencer, 1955.7.1. The armchair shows the squared-off *à l'anglaise* padding.

rounded shapes, such as those seen in the portrait of the comte d'Angiviller by Duplessis,[8] or that of the comte de Provence by Boze.[9] For the sofa, this technique was used only for the back. As mentioned in Capin's registers for the 1780s, the sides were "closed," that is, simply hung with a cloth and the covering fabric. Also according to Capin, the front edge of the platform and the horsehair seat cushion were stitched *à l'anglaise*. Since Bimont recommended making seat cushions between 16.2 and 27 cm tall,[10] we used the average height of 21.6 cm for the sofa cushion. Again following Bimont's advice, the pillows were cut 70.2 cm square and adorned with a tassel at each corner.[11]

The resulting ensemble reproduces the atmosphere of the Salon from the Hôtel de La Trémoille at the end of the 1780s. Every choice made for the upholstery of the room's furniture was based on historical references. To the extent possible, the numerous questions that arose during the planning and execution of this project were resolved by consulting contemporary models and pictorial or archival documentation.

NOTES

1. Paris, Mobilier National, inv. GMT 196. *Soieries de Lyon. Commandes royales au XVIIIe siècle (1730–1800)*. Lyon, Musée Historique des Tissus, December 1988–March 1989, cat. no. 61.
2. Ibid., cat. no. 62.
3. Ibid., cat. no. 91.
4. Amiens, Hôtel de Berny, inv. HB 141.
5. Los Angeles, J. Paul Getty Museum, inv. 88.DA.123.
6. Jean-François Bimont, *Principe de l'art du tapissier* (Paris, 1770), 17.
7. *Recueil de planches sur les sciences, les arts libéraux, et les arts méchaniques, avec leur explication* (Paris, 1771), 8th edition, vol. 9, pl. II, fig. 5.
8. Versailles, Musée du Château de Versailles, inv. MV 3926.
9. Hartwell House, near Aylesbury, Buckinghamshire, England.
10. Bimont, *Principe de l'art du tapissier*, 65.
11. Ibid., 68.

CONSERVATION OF THE *BOISERIE*

Lesley Bone

The broad aim of the conservation treatment for the Salon Doré from the Hôtel de La Trémoille has been to restore the room to its original plan, preserve all surviving elements from its initial installation in 1781, and return it, for the first time since its inception, to its original dimensions. Much of the extraneous modern addition, mainly on the east and west walls, which includes inbuilt display cases on the west wall—all of which were probably added in 1962 and 1995—has been removed, as have the results of many previous campaigns of restoration, which were well intentioned but often inaccurate. In addition, we have re-created, more accurately than in the room's previous incarnations, the pair of double-door glass windows on the west wall that originally opened onto a garden (see fig. 73).

Our conservation effort has revolved around the restoration of the paneling and doors, mirrors, and fireplace in addition to the furnishings, including the seating, chandelier, torchères, console, firedogs, porcelain vases, and clock. This account concentrates on the historical paneling, also known as the *boiserie*. As scant documentation exists for the restoration and reinstallation history of our paneling, most of our information has come from evidence found in the paneling itself and from the earliest photographic record of the room, from about 1905 (see fig. 4). We also studied similar rooms from the same period, such as the Grand Salon from the Hôtel de Tessé, installed at the Metropolitan Museum of Art, New York (see fig. 1), and the Salon Doré from the Hôtel de Clermont, at the Corcoran Gallery, Washington, DC (fig. 50). We hope that the conclusions we have drawn from these comparisons will extend conservation scholarship with respect to both our Salon and other period rooms.

A DESCRIPTION OF THE PANELING

The room's paneling, as it existed before conservation (see fig. 51), includes mirror cases that are the central focus of each wall. These consist of arched mirror frames topped by elaborate

FIG. 50. Jean-François-Thérèse Chalgrin (French, 1734–1811), Salon Doré from the Hôtel de Clermont, 1770. Corcoran Gallery of Art, Washington, DC, William A. Clark Collection.

carvings of wreaths and trophies. Each two-part mirror is held in place by an intricately carved and gilded inner frame. Four Corinthian pilasters, built with recessed right angles, anchor the corners of the room, while pairs of flat pilasters flank each mirror. Their bases rest on a chair rail that rings the room above the pedestals and dado. Four substantive door cases stand at either side of the mirrors on the south and north walls. Four narrow filler panels in these two walls, as well as two matching panels between the corner and central pilasters and the central extensions of both main panels of the east wall, appear to be later additions that we largely attribute to either the Salon's installation at La Dolphine in Hillsborough or its first installation at the California Palace of the Legion of Honor. In 1995, two sets of glass-fronted display cabinets were built into the west wall to display objects. The current project replaced these and re-created the window recesses on the west wall. Capping the room is the entablature, which consists of a frieze beneath a projecting cornice.

During the most recent deinstallation of the Salon, we noted that multiple placement references were written on the backs of the panels for the east and west walls. In comparing these notations with photographs of the Salon's previous installations at the Kahn residence and the Duveen Brothers galleries (see the timeline in this volume), it appears that the east and west walls were switched in those previous incarnations. Thus, the inscriptions refer to both positions.

Even more surprising, the mirror panel on the east wall bore the French inscription *en face du cheminée*—meaning that it originally belonged in the center of the north wall, opposite the south wall's chimneypiece. This switch must have taken place during the 1995 Legion installation, and we speculate that the reason for it was that as the long-sided east wall was the gallery's main focus, it would have been logical to place an original mirror in that prominent location.

The 1995 installation also raised the chair rail, which separates the upper paneling from the dado section, two inches higher than in the original design, creating a disproportionately high baseboard. The rail has now been lowered to its proper position, which restores the baseboard to a more proportionate six inches high.

FIG. 51. North wall of the Salon Doré before conservation treatment, 2012.

THE CONSTRUCTION OF THE PANELING

In the eighteenth century, paneled rooms were made by teams of craftsmen, each one with a specific, highly honed skill (see fig. 52). In a construction typical of its time, the Salon was lined with panels made of large oak timbers joined together sparingly with pegged mortise-and-tenon joints. Linden, a light, fine-grained wood, was selected for certain complicated carved decorative elements, such as the trophies, the floral wreaths, the cabling in the lower pilasters (also known as *chandelles*), and the laurel pendants below the acanthus scrolls flanking the doors. Linden enabled craftsmen to carve crisply detailed designs without chipping, and it also glues well to other woods, eliminating the necessity to secure the joint with wooden pegs. The original craftsmen went to great pains to keep the wood grain of adjoining sections running parallel to promote a stronger glue join.

FIG. 52. *Maniere de poser la menuiserie* (*Paneling Being Installed*) (detail), plate 99 in André-Jacob Roubo, *L'Art du menuisier*, vol. 1, pt. 2 (Paris, 1770). The Metropolitan Museum of Art, New York, The Thomas J. Watson Library.

After carving the wood, the craftsmen sized it by brushing the surface with parchment glue to create a good bond between the wood and the upper layers of gesso. Our analysis shows that the paneling has two layers of gesso, a mixture of glue and chalk that, once dry and sanded, produces a white surface that is very smooth. Gesso, however, also obscures the finer elements of the carving, requiring additional carving of the gesso itself to sharpen the design and restore such details as the veins and crisp edges of leaves.

Last, the craftsmen gilded the panels—a process in which the gesso is laboriously sanded to create a flawless surface, and then a thin yellow-ochre coating is applied to tone down the gesso's glaring white color. Should there be a break—charmingly known as a "holiday"—in the gold layer, this yellow ground would make the gap less obvious. Several applications of bole, a mixture of iron-rich clay and glue, follow, providing a slippery surface that can be easily burnished during the polishing stage (see fig. 53). Once the surface is perfect, the gilder loads a "gilder's mop," a special brush made of squirrel or goat hair that is widest near its tip, with water and passes it over the bole to reactivate the glue. At precisely the correct moment to ensure the gold will adhere properly—which an experienced gilder can judge by evaluating the exact gloss of a surface, which is affected by a variety of factors, such as temperature and humidity—the gilder takes a "tip," a very wide brush, just one to three squirrel hairs thick, brushes it across his or her face to create an electrostatic charge (which helps the gilder pick up the gold leaf, as the slightest air movement may cause it to crumple), and then places the tip on the surface of a micron-thick three-inch square of gold leaf. The charge lifts it

FIG. 53. Sample panel, prepared by Natasa Morovic, that shows the steps of the gilding process, from raw wood on the left to the final burnished gold surface on the right, 2013.

onto the brush, and then the gilder carefully lays the gold as flat as possible on the surface of the bole. Testing of our original panels revealed that they were gilded with 23-karat gold, alloyed with small amounts of silver and copper.[1] Our current conservation campaign used a gold of comparable purity (23.75-karat gold leaf) for the regilding.

The grand finale of any gilding process is the burnishing that gives the gold a dazzling reflectivity. The conservators on this project used highly polished agate stones for their burnishing, but in the eighteenth century a range of polishing stones was used, including porphyry. To help bestow dimensionality on certain features of the paneling, our gilders carefully chose which areas should receive a high burnish, such as the fluted indents in the pilasters, and which should remain matte, such as the flat reed interludes below the flutes. In doing so, our gilders followed the plan of the original gilders, who used their artistry to selectively apply a high burnish to certain areas, making them contrast brightly with the subtly textured matte areas, which recede (see figs. 54, 55). In both the Salon's original construction and its current restoration, once the gilding was completed, the room was painted.

THE SALON'S CONDITION BEFORE CONSERVATION

Before conducting treatments, museum conservators examined the room's elements. While deinstalling the paneling, they made the unexpected discovery that the capitals of the twelve pilasters are made of cast plaster rather than the more traditional carved wood. The Salon Doré at the Corcoran Gallery in Washington, DC, also

FIG. 54 (*left*). Detail of *chandelles* before treatment. Note the uniformly matte surface, with application of red bole visible. FIG. 55 (*right*). Detail of *chandelles* after treatment. Note the contrast of matte and burnished areas.

features plaster capitals, but documentation for that installation shows that they were made from molds derived from the room's wood capitals, which remain in their original site at the Hôtel de Clermont in Paris.[2] We have not found any documentary evidence to indicate that the Hôtel de La Trémoille capitals were derived from wood models, and in the photographs taken before the Salon's deinstallation at the Hôtel d'Humières (see figs. 4, 15), the capitals appear to be the same ones the room now holds. This suggests that the plaster capitals are probably original.

Conservators also examined the room's mirror casings, which are inlaid with "floating" parquetry (see the inventory in this volume), in which horizontal and vertical pieces are interlocked and inset into the framework, which holds the pieces together (see fig. 56). This technique is similar to that used for parquet floors.

Alterations and repairs had been made to the paneling since the Salon's inception. These interventions are evidenced by metal hardware, such as nails and screws, that were not part of the original construction and were used to fasten new wood restorations. Such structural repairs are also revealed by various types of wood that were utilized in place of the original oak, including pine, maple, red oak, and poplar. Repairs had also been made to the intricate trophy carvings: missing and broken sections often were re-created out of plaster or red oak, and, in most cases, they were carved and molded rather poorly, as the restorers lacked the confidence, detail, and rhythm of the original carvers.

Prior to our own treatment, the panels showed evidence of two earlier comprehensive water-gilding campaigns, with many intermittent, localized treatments in which both water and oil gilding were employed. During the past century, colored varnishes and different types of brass and mica paints were used to fill in areas of surface loss. The oldest existing layer of gold may be the original, since the techniques and materials utilized are consistent with those used in the 1780s; for instance, the color of the bole is a lighter orange-red than later applications. The second major gilding campaign, which employed a much thicker, darker, maroon-colored bole, is typical of nineteenth-century practice and may have been applied about 1879, when the room was transferred from the Hôtel de La Trémoille to the Hôtel d'Humières. It is clear that in this later comprehensive procedure, the original underlayers of gilding and bole generally were not removed, although perhaps some layers were taken off in surface cleaning to achieve a sound base for regilding.[3] In 1962 several new panels edged with gold bands were added to the room, presumably to match the original panels. It is probable that many of the bands in the original panels were regilded at this time to create a consistent appearance and that oil gilding was used: it does not require the laborious surface preparation of water gilding, but it produces a less lustrous gold surface.

FIG. 56. Mirror casing, showing parquetry construction, from ca. 1781.

FIG. 57. Detail of door before treatment.

Before our present conservation process, the gilded areas appeared patchy. Old repairs had darkened and dulled over time, and many surfaces were fragile. Overall cracking and flaking of paint and gold had compromised much of the smooth surface coherence of the original room (see fig. 57). Expediency, rather than concern for matching the careful craftsmanship of the original construction, seems to have guided most of the interventions since the last comprehensive water-gilding treatment of the late nineteenth century. One of the challenges we faced when developing the current treatment was that not all panels had suffered the same damages over time, and they had not been retouched uniformly.

CONSERVATION OF THE PANELING AND THE GILDING

Natasa Morovic (see fig. 58), conservator of frames and gilded surfaces at the Fine Arts Museums of San Francisco, led the gilding conservation effort, with help from contract conservator Deborah Bigelow, who has expertise in architectural gilding. They created a team of gilders and conservators who undertook the intensive restoration of the panels in a temporary conservation lab installed in the museum galleries (fig. 59). The treatment focused on returning the gilding to its original nuanced, high-quality execution. Ours was probably the second comprehensive campaign using only water gilding since the panels' creation, assuming that the lowest layer of gilding still present is indeed the original surface.

First we decided to strengthen and secure all the flaking and weak areas of the surface. Next we used various cleaning treatments to remove all

the patchy restorations until we reached a coherent water-gilded layer. Sometimes surfaces were compromised below this level, in which case we cleaned them farther down, to the gesso beneath the original gilding. More extensive removal, down to the wood, was required in some places, including one pilaster that had suffered severe water damage followed by mold growth in its gesso layer, which turned its entire surface quite dull and dark. We filled and sanded cracks and areas of loss in the wood, and we prepared sections to

FIG. 58 (*left*). Natasa Morovic, conservator of frames and gilded surfaces, using a gilder's tip to apply gold leaf to the upper decorative band of a door casing.

FIG. 59 (*below*). Temporary conservation laboratory installed in the Legion of Honor's Gallery 13. A large window was constructed for visitors to view the process.

FIG. 60. Detail of the carved wreath in the mirror trophy on the south wall partway through the conservation process. The gold surfaces have been cleaned, the old fills have been removed, the newly carved areas at the top of the wreath have been inserted, and smaller white gessoed areas await bole application prior to gilding.

be gilded following the traditional technique of water gilding: applying layers of gesso (see fig. 60) that we coated with bole before applying the 23.75-karat gold leaf. We followed stringent standards of surface preparation, including rigorous sanding protocols, to ensure that the final surface was perfectly smooth, achieving mirrorlike reflectivity. These new areas of gilding, where they are adjacent to older parts, were sometimes gently distressed to create a fluid visual transition.

We cleaned the nongilded sections of the paneling to remove grime, and sanded cracks and areas of loss to a smooth, paintable surface. Any cracks or loose joints were secured with adhesive, and, in some cases, old hardware was resecured to form tighter joins.

Once the panels were installed and lit, we evaluated the new gilding to see if any areas needed to undergo a process known as toning, which balances the appearance of the gold surfaces across the entire room. One intention of toning is to make some of the newly gilded surfaces slightly less shiny, but it can also subtly change the color of the gilding. Color matching begins in the early stages of the gilding process, as gilders choose a gold leaf that is as close as possible to the desired target color and then mix a bole color that further shifts the gold's tone into the required range (making it darker, lighter, greener, or redder). Despite this careful color matching at the start of the process, some toning is later applied through various techniques to achieve perfect integration and ensure harmony between old and new gilding—whether shiny or matte, light or dark—across the entire exterior of the paneling.

To restore the wood details, we relied on the skills of a master carver, Adam Thorpe (see fig. 61), who removed old repairs to the carved sections and replaced them with new wood passages informed by the paneling's original design and perspective. He selected a wood—*Tilia americana*, commonly known as American basswood, a close cousin of linden—to restore parts where the latter was originally used, such as in the raised carving of the wreaths and in the twisting and curling ribbon areas in the mirror trophies (see fig. 5). In areas of original oak carving, we employed oak for the restoration, too. Hide glue, a close approximation of the parchment glue that was originally used on the panels, was utilized to attach new

FIG. 61. Master carver Adam Thorpe using calipers to take measurements of the existing leaves so that he can re-create their dimensions in replicas used to fill areas of loss.

wood to old. Very occasionally, we used a modern wood epoxy for particularly difficult transitions in the complicated wreath composition, where the attachment would otherwise have been too tenuous.

DOORS

Five sets of double doors are presently associated with our Salon. The original room had four pairs of double doors, two sets each along the north and south walls, which created symmetry in the room. In 1781, three of these pairs were functioning doors; the fourth was a pair of blind, or nonfunctioning, doors at the southeast corner of the room. In the installation at the Hôtel d'Humières (see fig. 16) in 1879, the northeastern set was also converted to blind doors. The 1918 installation at the Otto Kahn mansion in New York (see fig. 13) included a modification to the east mirror frame that transformed it into a doorway that provided access to a corridor—this is the origin of the fifth set of doors. In the previous Legion installations, only two sets of doors were used, in the east corners of the north and south walls. The restored room now displays two additional sets of active doors—open for visitors to pass through—at the west corners of these walls.

Three pairs of doors have double-sided construction, meaning that the back of the door has an added door panel—making it twice as thick—that was finished to match the rooms adjacent to the Salon. These may have been added during the Rheems' installation of the *boiserie* at La Dolphine, but no drawings or photographs exist of the Salon or its adjoining rooms at this site, so we cannot be certain. The fourth set of doors is of single-sided construction, indicating that it was likely the blind pair originally located in the southeast corner of the room.

Each door features a small central panel with a finely carved, gessoed, and gilded frieze of arabesque vines and flowers silhouetted against a painted background (fig. 62). Only in these small central panels did we remove all of the paint down to the original gesso layer so as to set off the exquisite carving that was otherwise overwhelmed by multiple paint applications around it. We were able to clean the gilding of these areas down to a coherent gold surface that required very little regilding. The conservation treatment on the rest of the doors was similar to that on the paneling: we cleaned the paint surface and removed only the most recent paint layer, after which we filled and sanded any losses and cracks.

The lintel above each set of doors consists of a gilded plaster panel in which a design of arabesque curling vines echoes that in the doors' central panels. Each lintel is made in three sections and attached to the frame with forged square-headed nails inserted through the plaster. As conservators worked on the lintel of the southwest corner, scraping away the layers of paint, a puzzle emerged: this particular lintel was made in a completely different manner—on a pine board. It originally was painted and gilded in trompe l'oeil fashion, and then a section of arabesque scrolls, cast in plaster and backed with thick paper and strands of horsehair, was attached using multiple wire nails and gilded and painted to match the other lintels. Our initial speculation that this board was the "master" from which the others were produced was contradicted by its wire nails, which were not in common use until the mid-nineteenth century. Additional

FIG. 62. Detail of the central panel from one of the Salon's four doors during treatment, showing the highly detailed, gilded carving.

evidence suggests that at the time this board was made, the designs in the other panels were also modified—one vine leaf in this panel is mirrored by a similar element modeled over an earlier version in two of the other panels. It was unusual for the French to use pinewood, but this panel apparently was installed at the Hôtel d'Humières in Paris, as evidenced by the 1905 photographs of the Salon there.

PLASTER OVERDOOR RELIEFS

Above each door case, over the lintel and architrave, is a rectangular plaster overdoor panel cast in high and low relief. In a depiction that represents Love, two putti, seated in a garland of flowers, hold a medallion that shows a dancing nymph. Each original plaster exterior was coated some time during the past century with a thick dark gray paint. These reliefs are the same model as the set in the Grand Salon from the Hôtel de Tessé at the Metropolitan Museum of Art, New York. Metropolitan Museum scholars have indicated that the de Tessé panels were likely made by the sculptors Pierre Fixon and his son Louis-Pierre, craftsmen in eighteenth-century Paris who specialized in making plaster overdoor panels.[4] The Legion overdoors also may have been created by the Fixons. In the past, there has been some conjecture that the Legion overdoors were later copies of the de Tessé ones. This inference is not borne out in our examination, as the materials, aging of the surfaces, and method of manufacture, as well as the multiple restoration campaigns upon them, strongly suggest that these overdoors are contemporaneous to those in the Metropolitan Museum.

Since plaster is brittle, with a tendency to crack, the original craftsmen embedded thick hanks of reddish-brown flaxlike fibers into the material, which are visible on the back of the overdoor panels. X-rays revealed that wire was also embedded in the limbs of the putti to strengthen these vulnerable sections, most of which have nonetheless suffered damage. The makers also embedded a heavy iron structure into the rear of each relief to give dimensional support to the whole panel.

No documentary evidence of the original color of these plaster reliefs exists, but exploratory surface cleanings revealed a nuanced layer of distemper, a water-based paint, the color of limestone, which perhaps indicates they were painted to imitate stone. Water-soluble paint was the typical choice for painting highly carved areas, as it could be easily washed off between paintings, preserving the detail of the design. But in later years, this tradition was not followed on our plaster panels, which led to the carved details becoming obscured by layers of paint. Between the earliest paint wash and the latest gray paint layers, we found only faint traces of the intervening paint coats, including a white that was probably the color of the reliefs when they were installed at the Hôtel d'Humières.

Some detail in the central medallions had become indistinct, likely as a result of overzealous paint removal and, in a few cases, rather hurried repairs. This was particularly noticeable on the northeast panel, where modern tool marks and excessive filling of missing areas were evident. These old repairs often distorted the original alignment of the limbs of the putti. Our conservators removed old repairs, reintegrating the losses more sympathetically with the originals, and realigned the limbs more correctly. We reworked and sanded down old fills to match the texture of the original surface. An old glue that had been sloppily applied and had stained the adjoining surfaces proved to be quite difficult to dissolve, so we painted over these areas to lighten their dark tones. The paint on all of the panels was removed down to the early limestone-colored layer, and areas of fill and damage were painted to match (see fig. 63). We also restored the gilded bands at the bottom of each panel, which had darkened due to the tarnishing of earlier bronze overpainting.

THE ENTABLATURE AND CEILING ROSETTE

Above the main *boiserie* section of the room is the entablature, which consists of a horizontal plaster frieze and upper cornice band. The original French entablature did not make it across the Atlantic, so the paneling's installation at the Kahn mansion in New York was topped with a simple cornice molding. The current version dates from the Salon's 1962 installation at the California Palace of the Legion of Honor, prepared under that project's architect, Winfield Scott Wellington (see fig. 9). Wellington apparently had discovered the photographs of the Salon that were taken before it was removed from the Hôtel d'Humières in 1905, and he copied that design, with its cadence of frieze-cornice-frieze bands that ringed the top of the room.

The surface of the 1962 entablature was covered with a copper-zinc alloy leaf that was oil gilded. Such a technique is considerably cheaper and faster to apply than water gilding, but metal leaf does need to be coated with varnish to prevent it from tarnishing. In the 1995 reinstallation at the

FIG. 63. Overdoor treatment in progress, with the previous dark gray paint (*left*) being removed, revealing the limestone-colored surface beneath, and white areas of fill where past damage occurred (*right*).

Legion, the band's three sections were reduced to two—the upper frieze band was removed, presumably due to ceiling height restrictions in the new space and the compromised condition of some sections during their removal. With our new installation, a new cove was installed above the cornice.

The ceiling rosette has a history similar to that of the entablature; created for the 1962 installation at the Legion, it strongly resembles the eighteenth-century design visible in the photographs of the Salon from the Hotel d'Humières, from which it was presumably copied. It was removed from the Legion ceiling in 1990 and never replaced. Due to the complications of reinstalling such a heavy (over four hundred pounds) and unwieldy ceiling section in a seismically active zone, we decided to take molds from this version and make lightweight resin casts that were applied to the ceiling, gessoed, and oil gilded.

THE PAINT COLOR OF THE SALON

When exposed, the multiple coats of paint on the Salon's painted sections reveal the history of the room's color over time. In the lower reaches of the room, in areas such as the doors, which suffered daily wear and tear and were therefore painted frequently, there are at least twenty-two layers of color. Of course, we cannot know if any of these now-absent layers were removed in preparation for earlier repaintings, but it would have made economic sense to simply clean and repaint sound layers rather than removing them, especially considering that eighteenth-century paints left thinner coats than those used today.[5] Microscopic observation shows that even cleaning was often skipped, as dirt lines are visible between some layers.

Conservators examined the paneling to identify which area might retain the deepest sequence of paint colors hidden below. They found a section, tucked away in the bottom rail of one of the older doors, that likely held the secret of the very first paint color. A cross section of layers (fig. 64) revealed that the earliest one appeared to be a wonderfully buttery, waxy paint in almost perfect condition. There is documentation that Winfield Scott Wellington scraped the paint surface in 1960 and concluded that the room was originally this creamy yellow color[6]—which also appears to have been the basic shade used for the ten or so most recent layers in the life of the paneling before and after his discovery. To confirm these findings, we sent a sample to Dr. Susan Buck for analysis.[7]

Rather unexpectedly, Buck answered that this buttery layer was not paint at all, but a double layer of gesso applied to the wood. Presumably

FIG. 64. Magnified cross section of paint layers that were applied over gesso taken from the lower rail of one of the doors. The earliest layers are at the bottom and start with various shades of gray until about two-thirds up, as indicated by the arrow, when they transition from gray to a more yellowish color.

the parchment glue in the originally white gesso had yellowed over time and changed to its current creamy color. Buck, who has also analyzed the de Tessé room panels, confirmed that it was quite common for *boiserie* of this period to have been gessoed, even in areas that were to be painted, as it produced a smooth surface and prevented wood imperfections from showing through the paint layer. Additionally, gesso created a solid white base for a light-colored layer of paint and thus counteracted the dark underlying wood.

The layers of paint closest to the gesso in the analyzed sample appear to have been applied immediately after the gesso, as there is no dirt at this interface. These consist of two coats of a very porous and translucent light gray paint with the characteristics of a soft distemper. Jean-Félix Watin referred to the eighteenth-century preference for using cool-colored light gray paint to show off gold highlights to their greatest effect, as the inevitable yellowing of a white paint would create an undesirable contrast with gold leaf.[8]

Soon after the results of Buck's analysis were revealed, Xavier Bonnet discovered, at the Archives Nationales in Paris, an inventory of the objects found in the Salon in 1790, which was made upon the death of the duchesse de La Trémoille (see pp. 97–99 in this volume). An offhand comment in the middle of a sentence—"le pourtour du dit salon peint en gris rechampis en or" ("the wood paneling . . . of said salon painted gray and highlighted in gold")—helped to confirm that our analysis had revealed the initial paint color of the room.

The color of the Salon's paint seems to have remained constant over a long period of time, given the more than fifteen layers of light gray paint we see in some areas (such as the door rails). At some point—possibly during the New York installation at the Kahn residence—the color changed from gray to cream. That color trend continued, although the tone vacillated from slightly green to slightly orange, throughout later repaintings until the present restoration, which has returned the room to its original pale gray.

In the eighteenth century, paint colors did not have specific recipes. To change subtly the tone of white paint to a cooler hue, some painters used trace amounts of black from burnt vine stems, indigo, *noire de composition* (residues from the production of Prussian blue), or a combination of these ingredients. Paint was handmade by each painter, using unprocessed materials that often held a great variety of particle sizes. Differences among color batches, therefore, were quite common. The distemper in the original paint layer of our Salon is composed principally of chalk, with water, glue, and pigment. Knowledge of the properties of different chalks helped a painter to select the correct one: for example, *blanc de Bougival* was a white chalk that dissolved easily in water and was a top choice for distemper; the pigment would have been added to this white base. The other main ingredient, the glue, was typically a parchment size made by the painter from offcuts of calfskin from the glove-manufacturing trade. Since the glue was gelatinous when cold, the paint had to be heated, making the application process challenging.

With the help of paint technician Erika Sanchez-Goodwillie, we not only re-created the old distemper paint, using ingredients very similar to those originally employed, but also made a modern distemper that resembled the original in texture and sheen, utilizing a synthetic resin in place of animal glue. The advantage of this substitution was that we would not need to heat the paint before applying it, and the process would be much less labor intensive. Nevertheless, we still would have had to make the modern distemper from scratch, and it still would have been more challenging to apply than any commercially available paint. After exploring commercial paints that have qualities comparable to those of the old distemper paints, and after much debate, we decided to use a manufactured paint, matching the original color, that was also similar to the initial paint in both sheen and visual qualities (see figs. 65, 66). The manufactured paint would be easier than the re-created distemper paint for the paint contractors to handle, faster to apply within the limited time frame available for the work, and stand up better to the rigors of museum display.

FIGS. 65, 66. Door during and after treatment.

Beginning in the mid-eighteenth century, French taste in interior painting style appreciated a very matte, dry surface upon which brush marks were evident. Such an irregular surface bounces light in many directions, lending nuance to a paint color by softening its effect in the viewer's gaze. In contrast, gilding is confrontational: its high-sheen surface bounces light directly into the eyes. At the time of the Salon's creation, there was a sophisticated understanding of this interplay of surfaces and hence a demand for craftsmen who could produce it. The current restoration has made efforts to replicate this effect, both through the use of paint that incorporates texture and through the painting techniques.

The conservation of the Salon's paneling was achieved by our team of gilders, conservators, master carver, and painters, whose skills complement those of the original craftsmen. Sometimes the techniques and materials that we used were identical to those employed in the room's initial manufacture—as in the process of making the bole, in which we went so far as to obtain chalk from the area of Champagne, France, just as craftsmen would have done in 1781. At other times, we made small changes, such as using rabbit-skin glue rather than parchment (calfskin) glue, which is not commercially available. What unites the original makers and the current team is their dedication to perfection in every detail of their work, which is evident throughout the entire reinstallation of this period room.

NOTES

The installation and deinstallation of the paneling were carried out by our in-house technical and production staff, led by Julian Stark and Andrew Woodd of Atthowe Fine Art, who creatively negotiated many of the complexities of putting together all the sections that make up this room.—LB

1 Jason Anema and Kate Helwig, "Analysis of Samples for an 18th-Century Gilded Room," Canadian Conservation Institute (CCI) Report no. 5099, CCI125826, September 18, 2013.
2 Dare Myers Hartwell and Bruno Pons, *The Salon Doré* (Washington, DC, 1998), 49.
3 Natasa Morovic, e-mail communication, January 4, 2013.
4 Daniëlle Kisluk-Grosheide and Jeffrey Munger, *The Wrightsman Galleries for French Decorative Arts, the Metropolitan Museum of Art* (New Haven and London, 2010), 52.
5 Helen Hughes, senior architectural paint researcher, Building Research and Conservation Team, English Heritage, "Architectural Paint Research," *Context* 64 (December 1999).
6 In a letter to James W. Osgood dated October 24, 1963, about recent and proposed period room installations at the Legion, museum director Thomas C. Howe mentions both Winfield Wellington and that "paint scrapping [sic]" had taken place to reveal the original color. Registration Salon Doré file, 1959.123.2, Fine Arts Museums of San Francisco.
7 Dr. Susan L. Buck, "SFMFA French Period Room: Paint Analysis Phase I and Phase II," September 26, 2012, and May 3, 2013. Report Conservation Object files, Fine Arts Museums of San Francisco. Dr. Buck is a conservator specializing in the analysis of painted surfaces.
8 Jean-Félix Watin, *L'art du peintre, doreur, vernisseur*, first published in 1772.

du Roy Notaire au Chatelet de Paris soussigné
procedder a même Requete en presence que cy
devant a la Continuation du present Inventaire
ainsy qu'il suit

Dans un Salon ensuite de la Salle du Dais
ayant Vue sur le Jardin

Item un grand feu complet de fer poly a
l'ecurnement avec ornemens a Vase doré d'or moulu
en leur Surtout de fer blanc, deux bras de Cheminée
a trois branches garnis de leurs bobeches aussy de
Cuivre doré d'or moulu ; un Soufflet, un garde feu de
six feuilles de fer blanc ; deux petites battes de Cuir
le tout prisé cent Cinquante livres cy   150

Item trois grands Vases de porcelaine bleu
et blanche en dorée avec leurs Couvercles, deux
petites Girandoles de Cristal montées en Cuivre
doré d'or moulu sur leur pieds peints en façon de
laque ; deux autres Vases de Jaspe le tout faisant
Garniture de Cheminée prisés en ensemble la Somme
de Cent quarante quatre livres —   144

Item deux pieds ou Consoles de bois sculpté doré
a dessus de marbre blanc, deux pots de fleurs
artificielles d'auteurs Jaspe, des Jattes de
porcelaine sous leur Cage de Verre blanc prisés en ensemble
Vingt quatre livres Deux Cent livres cy   200

A l'égard d'une glace de Cheminée en deux
parties, la premiere de Soixante Six pouces de
haut la Seconde Cintrée de Vingt deux pouces aussy
de haut, toutes deux sur Cinquante de large

D'une autre glace au Trumeau en deux parties la
premiere de quatre Vingt deux pouces de haut,
la Seconde de Vingt Six deux pouces Cintrée aussy
de haut, toutes deux sur Cinquante de large

D'une autre glace en face de la Cheminée en
deux parties de même hauteur et largeur

The 1790 Inventory of the Salon

The French text is taken verbatim from the original document in the Archives Nationales, Paris.

INVENTAIRE DU SALON

Item un grand feu complet de fer poli à recouvrement avec ornement à vase doré d'or moulu et leur surtout de fer blanc, deux bras de cheminée à trois branches garnis de leurs bobèches aussi de cuivre doré d'or moulu, un soufflet, un garde feu de six feuilles de fer blanc, deux petits balais de crin le tout prisé cent cinquante livres, ci 150

Item trois grands vases de porcelaine bleue et blanche et dorées avec leurs couvercles, deux petites girandoles de cristal montées en cuivre doré d'or moulu sur leurs pieds peints en façon de laque, deux autres vases de jaspe le tout faisant garniture de cheminée prisés ensemble la somme de cent quarante-quatre livres, ci 144

Item deux pieds en console de bois sculpté doré a dessus de marbre blanc, deux pots de fleurs artificielles dans leurs jaspe de jattes de porcelaine sous leur cage de verre blanc prisé ensemble ~~vingt quatre~~ deux cent livres, ci 200

SALON INVENTORY

Item, a large complete fireplace set of polished iron, the firedogs each decorated with an ormolu vase and their *surtout* [cover] in white metal, a pair of three-branch wall lights with their bobeches also of brass gilded in ormolu, bellows, a six-panel white-metal firescreen, two small horsehair brooms, the whole appraised at one hundred fifty *livres* 150

Item, three large blue and white and gilded porcelain vases with their lids, two small crystal girandoles mounted in brass gilded in ormolu, their bases painted to imitate lacquer, two other jasper vases, the whole composing the mantelpiece garniture, appraised together at the sum of one hundred forty-four *livres* 144

Item, two console table legs of carved giltwood with a white marble top, two pots of artificial flowers in their porcelain bowls under their white glass case, appraised together at two hundred *livres* 200

A l'égard d'une glace de cheminée en deux parties, la première de soixante-seize pouces de haut, la seconde cintrée de vingt-deux pouces aussi de haut, toutes deux sur cinquante de large, d'une autre glace aussi en deux parties la première de quatre-vingt-deux pouces de haut, la seconde de vingt ~~six~~ deux pouces cintrée aussi de haut toutes deux sur cinquante de large, d'une autre glace en face de la cheminée en deux parties de même hauteur et largeur et d'une autre glace en entre-deux de croisée aussi en deux parties cintrée de même hauteur sur quarante-trois pouces de large sur leurs parquets et dans leurs baguettes et ornements de bois sculpté doré ainsi que la boiserie faisant le pourtour du dit salon peint en gris rechampis en or il n'e été du tout fait aucune prisée à la réquisition des parties et du dit sieur substitut comme étant posés à perpétuelle demeure et adhérant à l'hôtel pourquoi le présent article est ici tiré pour mémoire, ci . . . . mémoire

Item deux paires de bras de cheminée à trois branches chacune garnie de leurs bobèches le tout de cuivre doré d'or moulu prisé ensemble soixante-douze livres, ci 72

Item une pendule du nom de Ledunois à cadran d'émail marquant les heures minutes et secondes et les jours du mois de l'année dans sa boite et sur son pied à pilastre, figures et autres ornements de cuivre doré d'or moulu, prisée la somme de six cents livres, ci 600

Item seize chaises, six fauteuils de bois peint en gris couvert de velours d'Utrecht cramoisi prisés ensemble cent cinquante livres, ci 150

With respect to a fireplace mirror in two parts, the first seventy-six inches high, the second, arched, twenty-two inches high, both fifty inches wide; to another mirror also in two parts, the first eighty-two inches high, the second, arched, twenty-two inches high, both fifty inches wide; to another mirror opposite the fireplace in two parts of the same height and width and another mirror between the windows also in two parts, arched, of the same height by forty-three inches wide, on their parquets [backboards] and in their molding, and ornaments of carved giltwood as well as the wood paneling along the perimeter of said salon painted gray and highlighted in gold, no appraisal at all has been made at the request of the parties and of said *sieur substitut* [proxy for the duke or duke's representative] as their being permanently installed and attached to the *hôtel*, on account of which the present article is recorded here for reference . . . . reference

Item, two pairs of three-branch wall lights with their bobeches, the whole in brass gilded with ormolu, appraised together at seventy-two *livres* 72

Item, a clock with the name of Ledunois with an enamel face marking the hours, minutes, and seconds and the days of the month of the year, in its case and on its pilaster base, figures and other ornaments of brass gilded in ormolu, appraised at the sum of six hundred *livres* 600

Item, sixteen side chairs, six armchairs of gray-painted wood covered in crimson Utrecht velvet, appraised together at one hundred fifty *livres* 150

Item sept petits fauteuils en cabriolet de bois sculpté peint en gris dont quatre garnis chacun de leurs carreaux et les ~~qua~~ trois autres sans carreaux, trois chaises, douze fauteuils, deux bergères, une ottomane garnie de son coussin et deux carreaux, le tout de bois sculpté doré couvert de damas bleu et blanc, quatre chaises en prie-Dieu couvertes de velours d'Utrecht bleu et blanc, quatre parties de rideaux de croisée avec leurs pentes en guirlande de pareil damas, deux grandes housses de grosse toile jaune servant à couvrir les meubles, six petits écrans de bois d'acajou couverts de taffetas bleu le tout prisé ensemble la somme de huit cents livres, ci 800

Item deux tables de déjeuner de bois d'acajou en forme de guéridon et à dessus de marbre blanc à contour de cuivre doré prisé ensemble dix-huit livres, ci 18

Item un lustre de cristal blanc à douze branches prisé cent vingt livres, ci 120

Item, seven small cabriolet armchairs of carved wood painted gray, four of them upholstered with their seat cushions and the three others without cushions, three side chairs, twelve armchairs, two *bergères*, one sofa upholstered with its seat cushion and two pillows, the whole in carved giltwood covered in blue and white damask, four prie-dieu chairs covered in blue and white Utrecht velvet, four parts of window curtains with their festooned valences in the same damask, two large dust covers in coarse yellow cloth used to cover the furniture, six small mahogany screens covered in blue taffeta, the whole appraised together at the sum of eight hundred *livres* 800

Item, two mahogany breakfast tables with a pedestal base and a white marble top edged in gilt brass. appraised together at eighteen *livres* 18

Item, a twelve-branch white rock-crystal chandelier, appraised at one hundred twenty *livres* 120

Gallery

In April 2014 the newly renovated Salon Doré from the Hôtel de La Trémoille in the Legion of Honor was opened to the public. The photographs in this gallery show several details of the completed room.

(*left*) Detail of window curtains.

(*above*) Detail of carved giltwood laurel pendant flanking a doorway.

(*left*) Detail of pilaster with Corinthian capital.

(*above*) Detail of gilt bronze pinecone on chimneypiece.

(*below*) Upper portion of mirror frame, showing arch carved with coffering in perspective and a trophy comprising a floral wreath, sprays of laurel leaves, and symbols of Mercury.

(*facing*) Detail of mirror, pilaster, and gilt bronze wall light with its reflection (cat. no. 10).

(*above*) Detail of an armchair (*fauteuil à la reine*) (reproduction of cat. no. 6).

(*above right*) Detail of the giltwood basket of flowers underneath the console (cat. no. 4).

(*right*) Detail of carving on an armchair (reproduction of cat. no. 6).

(*facing*) Detail of valence of one of the window curtains and corner pilaster.

(*above*) Detail of painted plaster overdoor, depicting putti supporting a medallion with a dancing nymph.

(*left*) Detail of carved giltwood frieze of the console (cat. no. 4).

Checklist

Furnishings for the Salon Doré
at the Legion of Honor

The *salon de compagnie* had a strict furnishing program related to etiquette. It was for formal public entertaining, not private living. As the main reception room for an aristocratic household, it contained furniture that was grand rather than comfortable. The *mobilier d'architecture* usually consisted of a suite of eight to twelve armchairs and a sofa covered in silk damask or, more rarely, tapestry, which were placed around the walls and hardly, if ever, used or moved. The side chairs (*chaises courantes*, *volantes*, or *d'usage*) were placed in the middle of the room for visitors' use. The rest of the furniture generally was composed of giltwood consoles to complement the architecture, a chandelier, wall lights, firedogs, and a clock. Highly worked pieces of *ébénisterie* were confined to private apartments or rooms. Commodes, desks, and small tables were rarely placed in salons.

The furniture in the Salon Doré has been assembled using a variety of sources as guides, including the recently discovered room inventory of 1790 (see pp. 97–99 in this volume). We have attempted to display the Salon much as it would have been furnished in the eighteenth century, with a complement of chairs, a chandelier, wall lights, a garniture of blue vases, a clock, a pair of consoles, and a pair of firedogs.

Several pieces, including the wall lights, firedogs, and chandelier, were already in the Museums' collection, having been acquired for period rooms previously installed at the de Young. A surprisingly large number of the furnishings turn out not to be from the eighteenth century, as sold: the firedogs, formerly from the Wallace Collection, London; the wall lights, from Mrs. Cornelius Vanderbilt; and the glass chandelier are all nineteenth- and even twentieth-century examples. However, the torchères with figures by Jean-François Lorta are not only eighteenth century but appear to be of royal provenance, from the king of Sardinia.

Our reinstallation displays a group of *chaises* and *fauteuils*, a pair of *bergères*, and one *canapé*. Research has indicated that salons such as ours included as many as fifteen *sièges d'usage* (chairs for

FIG. 67. Henri-Pierre Danloux (French, 1753–1809), *The Baron de Besenval in His Salon de Compagnie*, 1791. Oil on canvas, 18¼ × 14⅝ in. (46.5 × 37 cm). National Gallery, London, bought 2004 (NG6598).

use), but that the Salon Doré contained ten. The seat furniture comprises a set of four *chaises courantes* in the Museums' collection, with the stamp of the Château de Saint-Leu, augmented by six of the same model, stamped by Georges Jacob and derived from the Rothschild mansion of Mentmore, later of the David-Weill Collection, Paris; a set of six *fauteuils* from the salon of Monsieur Périer's apartment in the Hôtel de Toulouse (now the Banque de France); and a pair of *bergères*, also featuring stamps by Georges Jacob. Two newly made armchairs and a *canapé* complete the set to get closer to the number of seats in the 1790 inventory. This collection of seating furniture will present a more accurate picture of how these *salons de compagnie* were furnished in Paris in the years before the Revolution.

The console was acquired especially for our Salon because its *goût grec* design elements and scale complement the architectural paneling of the room. Another, of a different width, was newly made to fit under the mirror so that the two consoles provide the necessary architectural elements of the Salon. We also obtained a gilt-bronze clock.

All of the upholstery and window coverings, executed by upholstery specialist and historian Xavier Bonnet, were manufactured to order based on documentary evidence he discovered at the Archives Nationales, Paris. The show covers of blue silk were woven by Tassinari & Chatel, Lyon (see fig. 46), to match a pattern of the 1780s, and blue *passementerie* was woven by Declercq to accord with eighteenth-century documents (see figs. 43, 44).

CHECKLIST

with Extracts from the Inventory of 1790

Texts in gray italics are extracts from the Inventory of 1790 (the English translation can be found with the original French text on pp. 97–99 in this volume).

EIGHTEENTH-CENTURY OBJECTS

1. Garniture of vases, 1768
   France
   Sèvres Porcelain Manufactory
   Soft-paste porcelain
   Gift of Archer M. Huntington
   1927.184a–b, 185a–b, 186a–b

   trois grands vases de porcelaine bleue

The French royal factory at Sèvres produced highly decorated vases for display in luxury interiors. Often made in pairs or larger sets (known as garnitures), they provided an important decorative element in the sumptuous schemes of interior decoration. The gilded areas on these porcelains simulate gilt-bronze mounts. As seen in the 1791 portrait by Henri-Pierre Danloux of the baron de Besenval in his *salon de compagnie* (fig. 67), porcelains such as these were prominently displayed on mantelpieces, commodes, and consoles. Their colors and the decorative motifs of the gilt-bronze mounts frequently complemented the architecture and fabrics of a room.

Such objects were created under the direction and design of the *marchand-merciers*, dealers of luxury goods who operated from shops in fashionable quarters of eighteenth-century Paris and collaborated with various makers, such as the Sèvres manufactory and bronze workers, to create magnificent works for their clients.

This garniture of three vases is decorated with the *encrusté* technique, whereby the ground color was scraped off after firing to provide a white ground for decoration. The motif of flowers and fruit on the fronts and backs is framed by floral garlands, all on a *bleu fallot* ground overlaid with *oeil-de-perdrix* ("eye of the partridge") gilding. The ornate effect of the gilding was achieved through several applications of gold powder and binder to the surface of the soft-paste porcelain and firing at a low temperature. The gilding was then polished with a hard stone, such as agate, and ornamental elements, such as the basket-weave pattern on the stand and the egg-and-dart pattern on the lid rim, were tooled onto the surface. Although the Sèvres archives contain no documentation for these vases, it is known that the decoration of such objects often harmonized with the paneling of the room for which they were intended. The fine painting on the backs indicates that these pieces were originally displayed against a mirror, on top of a console or mantelpiece.

2. Pair of vases, ca. 1780
France
Sèvres Porcelain Manufactory
Hard-paste porcelain and gilt-bronze mounts
Gift of Dorothy Spreckels Munn
Reputedly made for Château de Randan
1978.11.1a–b

3. Mantel clock, ca. 1780
France
Jean-André Lepaute, clockmaker
(French, 1720–1789)

Gilt bronze, enamel, glass, metal, and ebonized wood
Signed on dial: *Lepaute/H.ger DU ROI*
Museum purchase, European Art Trust Fund
2013.5a–b

une pendule du nom de Ledunois à cadran d'émail marquant les heures minutes et secondes et les jours du mois de l'année dans sa boite et sur son pied à pilastre, figures et autres ornements de cuivre doré d'or moulu

Lepaute was a business run by the brothers Jean-André and Jean-Baptiste Lepaute. They worked as clockmakers to the king until the fall of the monarchy in 1792, although by that date Jean-André had died. As royal suppliers, they had a workshop in the Louvre gallery, which meant they could work outside guild restrictions, but because it was so small they had another, larger workshop nearby in the place du Palais-Royal, where this clock was probably made.

A clock of this model was delivered in 1779 for the substantial sum of 5,000 *livres* (nearly five times the annual income for a skilled laborer at the time) to the comte d'Artois, brother of King Louis XVI, for Bagatelle, his country house near Paris. It is designed with a group of winged putti playing with a celestial globe, representing Astronomy, set above an architectural case decorated with heavy laurel garlands hanging from brackets. The gilt bronze is finished to the highest degree of richness, with precise modeling and meticulous chasing—the best of which is evident in the rippled edges of the laurel leaves and the texture of the clouds. Lepaute is known to have used the finest *bronziers* and gilders of the day, and this care is apparent in the exceptional quality of the case of this clock.

4. Console table, ca. 1780
   France
   Giltwood and marble
   Museum purchase, European Art Trust Fund
   2013.4a–b

deux pieds en console de bois sculpté doré

This gilded wood console, composed of scrolling bracket supports and decorated with heavy floral garlands, is typical of the early Louis XVI period. Such pieces of furniture were devised in the 1770s and 1780s to fulfill an architectural role in the grander rooms of Parisian mansions and were firmly engaged with the paneling in the rooms. This table has strong affinities with a drawing after the designer Richard de Lalonde (French, 1738–1805) (see fig. 7).

This variation on the Neoclassical style of decoration is also found in our Salon. The large-scale acanthus foliage motif, the egg-and-dart border, and the fluting of the legs are used in the paneling of the room as well, along with the floral carvings on the garlands and wreaths. In addition, the console has a white marble top similar to that used in the chimneypiece—an important method of achieving harmony in the French eighteenth-century interior. This console is particularly suited for the window wall of the Salon; its proportions and complementary decorative scheme enhance its role as the most significant architectural furniture in the room.

5. Pair of torchères, 1788
   France
   Jean-François Lorta (French, 1752–1837), sculptor
   Gilt bronze, white marble, and porphyry
   Signed and dated on base:
   JOAN FR. LORTA Sculp 1788
   Museum purchase, Mildred Anna Williams Collection
   1962.38–39

These white marble torchères take the forms of female figures, representing Spring and Autumn, each holding a torch that supports three gilt-bronze lights festooned with swags. Both pieces were badly damaged in the Loma Prieta earthquake of 1989 and were lacking the upmost *athénienne* tripods. In anticipation of the Salon renovation, the torchères were recently restored and the *athénienne* tripods recast from models in the collection of the Musée du Louvre, Paris.

Reported to have been made for the king of Sardinia, whose sisters married the brothers of Louis XVI, these torchères are related to four at the Louvre that were supplied to Mesdames Tantes for the Château de Bellevue.

CHAIRS

6. Set of six *fauteuils*, ca. 1786
   France
   Carved and gilded walnut
   Inscribed on labels on the back rails:
   Pour le Salon de Monsieur Perrier [sic]
   Museum purchase, European Art Trust Fund
   2012.28.1–6

   *douze fauteuils . . . de bois sculpté
   doré couvert de damas bleu et blanc*

These armchairs (*fauteuils à la reine*) were made for the salon of a Parisian aristocratic mansion. Designed in the high Louis XVI style, with wide seats and rectangular straight backs, they were intended for arrangement around the walls of the room, as part of the *mobiliers meublantes* or *mobiliers d'architecture*. Meant more for display than for use, such grand chairs were intended to reflect the status of their owner and work in tandem with the paneling to create a decorative effect. These armchairs represent the most refined level of chair making in Paris during the 1780s. Their rectangular backs were created by a *menuisier* (joiner), then meticulously carved by a specialist, who crafted the delicate Neoclassical ornamentation: garlands of laurel, sprays of ivy, ropes, pearls, and acanthus foliage.

Delivered around 1786, these armchairs—as the labels on the back rails inform us—were intended for the salon of Guillaume Périer, vicomte de Grèzes, a successful lawyer and businessman who was the general administrator for estates of the duc de Penthièvre, a cousin of King Louis XVI. Périer had an eleven-room apartment in Penthièvre's Hôtel de Toulouse, one of the grandest houses in Paris, which is today the headquarters of the Banque de France. The armchairs were once part of a much larger suite of some eighteen seats, including a sofa, a pair of marquises, and several side chairs.

7. Set of six *chaises*, ca. 1780
   France
   Carved and gilded walnut
   Stamped: *G. Jacob* (French, 1739–1814)
   Museum purchase, European Art Trust Fund and Anonymous Gift
   2012.45.1–6

*trois chaises . . . de bois sculpté doré
couvert de damas bleu et blanc*

These side chairs (*chaises en cabriolet*) were made for the salon of a grand French house and were designed in the high Louis XVI style with wide oval seats and curved backs in the form called *cul de four* (horseshoe). They were intended for arrangement in a U in the center of the room for visitors' use (see fig. 22).

The chairs are delicately proportioned. Their curved backs were fashioned by the noted *menuisier* Georges Jacob and then exquisitely carved with refined Neoclassical details by a craftsman. These pieces have a distinguished provenance: they were part of the Rosebery Collection at Mentmore, the English mansion of the Rothschilds, and later the David-Weill Collection, Paris.

8. Set of four *chaises*, ca. 1780
France
Carved and gilded wood
Stamped with the brandmark of the
Château de Saint-Leu
Gift of Mrs. Clarence Sterling Postley
2009.4.10.1–4

*sept petits fauteuils en cabriolet
de bois sculpté peint en gris*

Of the same model as the set of six side chairs above, these four chairs have a royal provenance, deriving from the Château de Saint-Leu in the 1780s, owned by the duchesse d'Orléans, who was the daughter of the duc de Penthièvre. They appropriately (for our purposes) bear labels inscribed *Chaise Courante du Salon*.

9. Pair of *bergères*, late eighteenth century
France
Carved and painted wood
Stamped: *G. Jacob* (French, 1739–1814)
Gift of Mrs. Clarence Sterling Postley
2009.4.5.1–2

*deux bergères . . . de bois sculpté doré
couvert de damas bleu et blanc*

Similar in design yet simpler than the frames set of the armchairs made for Monsieur Périer, these sumptuously upholstered *bergères* were intended to be positioned next to the chimneypiece, where they provided the most comfortable seats for the honored guests and the mistress of the house.

OBJECTS FROM THE NINETEENTH CENTURY OR LATER

Sold in 1955 by French & Company as eighteenth-century models by Jean-Charles Delafosse (French, 1734–1789), these wall lights are now recognized as late-nineteenth- or early twentieth-century copies. They have hollow branches for electrical wiring and were previously a fixture in the music room of Mrs. Cornelius Vanderbilt's Fifth Avenue mansion in New York.

10. Four wall lights, nineteenth century or later
    France
    Gilt bronze
    Museum purchase, Roscoe and
    Margaret Oakes Collection
    55.41.19–22

    *deux paires de bras de cheminée à trois
    branches chacune garnie de leurs bobèches
    le tout de cuivre doré d'or moulu*

According to the 1790 inventory, the fireplace mantel was ornamented with a porcelain garniture and flanked with a pair of three-branched wall lights. The two further arched mirror cases were also flanked by a pair of gilt-bronze wall lights. These three-branch wall lights each consist of a fluted and floral swag–decorated back plate surmounted by an acanthus-leaf finial. Each arm terminates in a circular bobeche and a single candle socket.

11. Pair of firedogs with flaming tripod cassolettes, nineteenth century
    France
    Gilt bronze
    Museum purchase, Roscoe and
    Margaret Oakes Collection
    55.41.23

    *un grand feu complet de fer poli à recouvrement
    avec ornement à vase doré d'or moulu*

At the center of each of these andirons is a flaming tripod cassolette applied with three goat heads,

supported on a pedestal with a mask of Apollo and surrounded with *rinceaux* (scrollwork), drapery swags, and a seed-pod finial at each end. Our example lacks a plinth.

Possibly designed after an eighteenth-century model by the *bronzier* Claude-Jean Pitoin (French, active ca. 1777–1784; identification made by Dell, *The Frick Collection*, 250), these firedogs were purchased from French & Company in 1955 with a provenance of the Elbert H. Gary Collection and William Randolph Hearst. They are reputed to have come from Sir John Murray Scott and the Wallace Collection.

12. Chandelier, second quarter of twentieth century
France
Glass and gilt bronze
Gift of Dr. and Mrs. Sidney Newcomer
1999.77
un lustre de cristal blanc à douze branches

This chandelier entered the Fine Arts Museums' collection as an eighteenth-century object. Since that time, it has been recognized as having been made in the second quarter of the twentieth century, in the style of 1780.

—*Maria Santangelo*

Timeline

This Salon was originally installed as the *salon de compagnie* in the Hôtel de La Trémoille in 1781. It was the main reception room in the duchesse de La Trémoille's apartments of this aristocratic mansion, situated on rue Saint-Dominique on the Left Bank of Paris. The Salon remained the centerpiece of the Hôtel de La Trémoille throughout the Revolution and into the nineteenth century. Then, in 1877, the *hôtel* fell victim to the urban remodeling of Paris. Moved first to the nearby Hôtel d'Humières, the Salon then crossed the Atlantic to the United States in the early twentieth century. From 1879 to 1995, the *boiserie* (carved and gilded paneling) from the Salon was moved at least six times.

FIG. 68. The Hôtel d'Humières, Paris, ca. 1905, before the building's demolition, showing the three windows of the Salon at left on the ground floor. Société d'histoire et d'archéologie du VIIe arrondissement de Paris.

1781 The Salon is installed in the Hôtel de La Trémoille (see figs. 17, 29, 32–36), rue Saint-Dominique (formerly the Hôtel de Neuchâtel, de Béthune, and de Châtillon). It was designed for Jean-Bretagne-Charles, duc de La Trémoille et de Thouars (1737–1792), and his second wife, Marie-Maximilienne, princess of Salm-Kyrburg.

1877 The Hôtel de La Trémoille is demolished for the building of the boulevard Saint-Germain. The owner, the marquise de Croix, removes the paneling and takes it with her to her new home, the Hôtel d'Humières (fig. 68).

1879 The *boiserie* of the Salon is installed overlooking the garden on the ground floor of the Hôtel d'Humières, rue de Lille.

FIG. 69. The Salon Doré installed in Duveen Brothers' showroom, 1946–1947.

1905　The Hôtel d'Humières is torn down to make way for several apartment buildings. This demolition causes concern, and the Société d'histoire et d'archéologie du VIIe arrondissement de Paris extensively photographs the *hôtel* and its Salon.

1918　Otto Kahn mansion, 1 East 91st Street, New York (see figs. 13, 14). The *boiserie* is installed as the "French salon" at the center of Kahn's massive new home, largely in its original footprint but with some of the room's original elements altered.

1934　Duveen Brothers, 720 Fifth Avenue, New York. After Kahn's death, his widow sells the room to Duveen Brothers. It is installed as one of the art dealer's main showrooms (figs. 12, 69) by the decorating firm of Alavoine. The paneling and the dimensions of the Salon are greatly changed.

1955–1958   Richard Rheem, La Dolphine, Burlingame, California. The *boiserie* is sold to Mr. Rheem by Duveen as being from the more famous Hôtel de Crillon, and by the equally famous architect Ange-Jacques Gabriel—a spurious provenance. It is installed as a ballroom in Rheem's home, La Dolphine, by the Parisian decorating firm of Decour.

1962   Legion of Honor, San Francisco. The Salon is accepted as a gift from Mr. Rheem and his wife in 1959 on the advice of the architectural historian John Harris. University of California, Berkeley, professor Winfield Scott Wellington researches the room and rediscovers its earlier provenance in the Hôtel d'Humières and advises on its installation in Gallery 7 of the Legion of Honor. The Salon is restored to its apparently original dimensions of about thirty by thirty feet (see fig. 70).

1990   Legion of Honor, San Francisco. The Salon in Gallery 7 is deinstalled as part of the comprehensive building seismic retrofit undertaken during the early 1990s.

FIG. 70. This photograph from 1983 documents the first installation of the *boiserie* of the Salon Doré at the Legion of Honor.

1995   Legion of Honor, San Francisco. The Salon is reinstalled in Gallery 11 as part of the retrofit of the 1990s (fig. 71). It is shown as a "paneled environment," without parquet flooring, ceiling, windows, or two pairs of its doors. New showcases replace the windows.

FIG. 71. The 1995 installation of the Salon Doré at the Legion of Honor, photographed in 2012.

FIGS. 72, 73. Renderings by Andrew Skurman Architects of the east wall (*top*) and west wall (*bottom*) of the renovated Salon Doré, 2013.

2014 Legion of Honor, San Francisco. The Salon is newly installed with its paneling conserved and architectural elements reinstated (see figs. 72, 73; see also the gallery in this volume). New windows and ceiling, plus a parquet de Versailles, are added. The original square form is restored. A new furniture scheme is also installed, with armchairs, side chairs, *bergères*, and a *canapé* upholstered in blue silk, as well as two console tables and new lighting that uses the historical fixtures.

—*Maria Santangelo*

Selected Bibliography

Archives Nationales, Paris. T//1051/55. *Papiers La Trémoille. Mémoire des ouvrages de peinture et dorure par supplément pour le service de Monseigneur le duc de La Trémoille en son hôtel rue Saint-Dominique, sous les ordres et conduite de monsieur Delapoize architecte, par Royer fils peintre et doreur en bâtiment demeurant rue du Four faubourg Saint-Germain, dans le courant des années 1782, 83, 84, 85, 86 et 87.*

Bizardel, Yvon. *Hôtel de La Trémoille, rue de Vaugirard.* Alençon: Imprimerie Alençonnaise, 1979.

Blondel, Jacques-François. *L'Architecture françoise . . . Paris, 1752–1756.* 4 vols. Paris: Pascal et Gaudet, 1904.

De Châtillon de La Trémoille Tarente, Louise-Emmanuelle. *Souvenirs de la princesse de Tarente, 1789–1792.* Nantes: Émile Grimaud et fils, imprimeurs-éditeurs, 1897; Paris: Honoré Champion, 1901.

Dell, Theodore. *The Frick Collection: An Illustrated Catalogue*, vol. 6: *Furniture and Gilt Bronzes, French.* Princeton, NJ: Princeton University Press, 1992.

Le faubourg Saint-Germain: La rue Saint-Dominique: Hôtels et amateurs. Paris: Délégation à l'action artistique de la Ville de Paris, Société d'histoire et d'archéologie du VIIe arrondissement de Paris, 1984.

Gady, Alexandre. *Les hôtels particuliers de Paris du Moyen Âge à la Belle Époque.* Paris: Éditions Parigramme, 2008.

Harris, John. *Moving Rooms: The Trade in Architectural Salvages.* New Haven and London: Yale University Press, 2007.

Hartwell, Dare Myers, and Bruno Pons. *The Salon Doré.* Washington, DC: Corcoran Gallery of Art, 1998.

Kisluk-Grosheide, Daniëlle, and Jeffrey Munger. *The Wrightsman Galleries for French Decorative Arts, the Metropolitan Museum of Art.* New Haven and London: Yale University Press, 2010.

La Trémoille, Louis, Antoine Joseph Philippe Walsh Serrant, Charles François du Périer Dumouriez, and Louis Dieusie. *Souvenirs de la révolution: Mes parents.* Paris: Société anonyme de publications périodiques, 1901.

Mairie du 7ème arrondissement, Paris. *Bulletin de la Société d'histoire et d'archéologie du VIIe arrondissement de Paris*, no. 1 (March 1906).

Metropolitan Museum of Art. *Period Rooms in the Metropolitan Museum of Art.* New York: Harry N. Abrams, Inc., Publishers, 1996.

Munger, Jeffrey. "French Upholstery Practices of the 18th Century." In *Upholstery in America and Europe from the Seventeenth Century to World War I*, ed. Edward S. Cooke Jr. New York: W. W. Norton, 1987, 120–147.

Ouziel, Fabrice. "Le grand appartement de l'hôtel de Saint-Florentin." *L'Estampille/L'Objet d'art*, no. 438 (September 2008): 126–136.

Pons, Bruno. *Architecture and Panelling: The James A. de Rothschild Bequest at Waddesdon Manor.* London: Philip Wilson Publishers Limited, 1996.

———. *French Period Rooms, 1650–1800: Rebuilt in England, France, and the Americas.* Dijon: Éditions Faton, 1995.

La rue de Lille: Hôtel de Salm. Paris: Délégation à l'action artistique de la Ville de Paris, Société d'histoire et d'archéologie du VIIe arrondissement de Paris, 1983.

Scott, Katie. *The Rococo Interior: Decoration and Social Spaces in Early Eighteenth-Century Paris.* New Haven and London: Yale University Press, 1995.

Tate, Susan Douglas, Linda Stevenson, and Fabrice Ouziel. *Concorde: Hôtel de Talleyrand, George C. Marshall Center: United States Department of State, 2, rue Saint-Florentin, Place de la Concorde, Paris: A Commemorative Edition.* Gainesville: University of Florida Publications Office, 2007.

Verlet, Pierre. *The Eighteenth Century in French: Society, Decoration, Furniture.* Rutland, VT, and Tokyo, Japan: Charles E. Tuttle Company, 1967.

Whale, Winifred Stephens. *The La Trémoille Family.* Boston and New York: Houghton Mifflin Company, 1914.

—*Maria Santangelo*

Acknowledgments

I wish to extend gratitude to the many contributors who have made this renovation and its accompanying scholarly programming possible.

At the Fine Arts Museums of San Francisco, I thank Colin B. Bailey, director of museums, for his enthusiasm for this project, and Diane B. Wilsey, president of the Board of Trustees, who has been a great supporter of this renovation from its inception. I also thank Richard Benefield, deputy director; Michele Gutierrez-Canepa, chief financial officer and foundation fiscal officer; Patricia Lacson, director of facilities; and Julian Cox, founding curator of photography and chief administrative curator. Further thanks are extended to Krista Brugnara, director of exhibitions; Therese Chen, director of collections management; Lisa Podos, director of strategic projects; and their teams for all of the work that they have put into this presentation.

My gratitude is given to the other authors of this book, who have shared their expertise. From the beginning of this project, Alexandre Pradère has offered his advice; he also contributed his entrancing essay for this volume. The expert on historic upholstery Xavier Bonnet undertook extensive research for us, including his unveiling of the 1790 inventory, which has transformed this project and is detailed in his essays herein. Lesley Bone, head of objects conservation for the Museums, not only led the renovation, but also provided a fine essay that describes the technical aspects of restoring the historic paneling. And Maria Santangelo, associate curator of European decorative arts and sculpture, helped at every stage to bring this elaborate project to fruition, including her important contributions to this publication.

I further thank Leslie Dutcher, director of publications, and Danica Michels Hodge, editor, for ably overseeing this catalogue with the assistance of Laura Harger, editor; and Sue Grinols, director of photo services, who managed much of the new photography. I am also grateful to Wilsted and Taylor Publishing Services, including Christine Taylor, Melody Lacina, Yvonne Tsang, and Jennifer Uhlich, for their help in producing this book, with special mention to Evan Winslow Smith for his assistance with the color proofing. Further thanks are owed to Rose Vekony for her fine translations of the many French texts in this catalogue, and to Henrik Kam and Randy Dodson for shooting much of the photography found in these pages. I also thank Friesens for the quality printing of this publication. This book could not have been realized without the support of the European Decorative Arts Council (EDAC) and the Andrew W. Mellon Foundation Endowment for Publications. In addition to the printed catalogue, many elements from this scholarship have been further shared with our audiences through electronic media, thanks in large part to Sarah Bailey Hogarty and Brinker Ferguson in the Museums' marketing department. Gratitude is also extended to the Samuel H. Kress Foundation.

For the conservation under Lesley Bone's leadership, I thank the numerous skilled conservators and artisans who spent many hours restoring our Salon. For the paneling, Natasa Morovic, the Museums' conservator of frames and gilded surfaces, ran the conservation studio, where many assisted in the elaborate gilding process, including Deborah Bigelow, Richard Boerth, Danielle Boiardi, and Nancy Thorn. Adam Thorpe brought his skills as master carver to repair parts of the paneling. Further thanks are extended to the greater conservation team: Tegan Broderick, Jessica Burkhart, Catherine Coueignoux, Emma Drew, Susan Jackson, Sarah Johnson, Emy Kim, Connie Levathes, Thomas Nguyen, Benedicte Nilssen, Kristi Parenti-Kurttila, Marlene Raedisch, and Museums' trustee Lisa Sardegna. Erika Sanchez-Goodwillie aided us in the painting composition and testing. Craig Harris, manager of installation and preparation at the Fine Arts Museums, and his team of technicians helped with many aspects of the Salon renovation, ably assisted by Andrew Woodd from Atthowe Fine Art Services. Elisabeth Cornu, former conservator at the Fine Arts Museums, also aided us in the early stages of this undertaking.

This project could not have happened without the services of Andrew Skurman as architect, along with William Hull and Paul Hayes. Kenneth Paige of Paige Glass and Tim Folger of Folger & Burt Architectural Hardware, Inc., also contributed their efforts to our endeavor. In Paris, I am grateful to Benjamin Steinitz for his advice and support, for his donation of a parquet floor, and for managing much of the conservation project in France; Pierre Olivier Chanel, who gave us a beautiful mirror for the Salon; Marc Bascou and his colleagues in the works of art department at the Musée du Louvre, who allowed us to copy lost sections of the Lorta torchères; Nicolas Personne for his research; and conservation architect Fabrice Ouziel for his counsel. In Los Angeles, Gillian Wilson was always ready with advice; Charissa Bremer-David, curator, and Brian Considine, chief conservator, at the J. Paul Getty Museum generously helped us on this project; and Teresa Morales undertook essential delving into the Carlhian Records and the Duveen Brothers Records. In London, the architectural historian John Harris, who originally advised on the acquisition of the Salon in 1959, offered us his extensive counsel; Dame Rosalind Savill provided important insights; and Sarah Medlam, formerly of the Victoria and Albert Museum, generously gave us helpful advice on the display of period rooms. I also thank Daniëlle Kisluk-Grosheide at the Metropolitan Museum of Art, New York, for allowing us access to their object files and for her advice and encouragement in renovating the Salon; her colleagues in the conservation department also provided support. At the Musée Historique des Tissus in Lyon, Maximilien Durand is thanked for permitting the reproduction of the silk fabric, and at the Musée de l'Hôtel de Berny and Musée de Picardie in Amiens, François Lernout is gratefully acknowledged for allowing the reproduction of the *passementeries*. Further thanks are given to Ulrich Leben, curator at Waddesdon Manor, Brigitte Gournay, Robert Domergue, and our colleague Louise Chu.

Our Salon and its accompanying program could not have been realized without the generous funding of our many patrons. I thank Cynthia Fry Gunn and John A. Gunn, who are the principal donors, and the members of EDAC and Friends of the Fine Arts Museums, who have supported this project throughout its many stages. Further thanks are given to our corporate sponsor, Breguet. And last, but not least, I thank Adolphus Andrews Jr. for his passion for this project since its provenance. I dedicate this catalogue to him.

—*Martin Chapman*

About the Contributors

MARTIN CHAPMAN is curator in charge of European decorative arts and sculpture at the Fine Arts Museums of San Francisco. His recent exhibitions and publications include *Marie-Antoinette and the Petit Trianon at Versailles* and *Royal Treasures from the Louvre: Louis XIV to Marie-Antoinette*.

ALEXANDRE PRADÈRE is an art historian and an expert on French furniture. His publications include *French Furniture Makers: The Art of the Ébéniste from Louis XIV to the Revolution*, a monograph on Charles Cressent, and numerous articles on such subjects as collectors, Parisian and country houses, and the successors of André-Charles Boulle the Elder.

XAVIER BONNET is an art historian and an expert on historic upholstery techniques and textile decoration. He was a fellow at the Académie de France in Rome in 2010–2011, and was awarded grants from the Getty Research Institute and the Winterthur Museum in 2006 and 2012, respectively.

LESLEY BONE is head objects conservator at the Fine Arts Museums of San Francisco. She has worked on many restoration treatments at the Museums, including artworks from the Saxe, Friede, and Scheller collections, and she oversaw the conservation of the Salon Doré at the Legion of Honor.

MARIA SANTANGELO is associate curator of European decorative arts and sculpture at the Fine Arts Museums of San Francisco. Since joining the department in 2007, she has managed the reinstallation of the Porcelain Gallery at the Legion of Honor and has assisted Chapman with numerous publications and exhibitions.

Index

Page numbers in **bold** refer to illustrations.

Alavoine decorating firm, 21, 113
Alembert, Jean le Rond d', 74
Allen, Philippe-Bernard, 54
Angiviller, comte d', 75
appartements. See rooms
Archives Nationales, Paris, 93, 103
armchairs: formal vs. utilitarian, 38; social life facilitated by, 9, 11, 38–39, 46. See also *bergères*
armchairs in the Hôtel de La Trémoille (1790 inventory), 55, 56, 60, 61, 62, 63, 64, 65, 72, 74, 98–99
armchairs in the Salon Doré: at Hôtel de La Trémoille, 13, 60; at Legion of Honor (2014), 7, 9, 11, 102–103, 108, **108**, 115
Artois, comte d', 106
audience rooms (*salles du dais*), **2**, 26, 29, 52, 56, 60, 63, 65, 66
Auerbach Glasow French lighting company, 7
Aumont family, 66n23

Banque de France, 47n6, 103, 108
Bastille, demolition of, 33n25
Beauvau, Marshal de, 40, **40**
Bélanger, François-Joseph, **10**
Bellat, Jean, 67n31
Bellegarde, Moravan de, 43
Belle-Isle, Marshal de, 37
bergères, 11, 39, 54, 60, 61, 62, 63, 64, 72, 99, 102, 103, 109, **109**, 115
Bernard, Samuel, 15n16
Besenval, baron de, **48**, 103, 105
Bigelow, Deborah, 84
Bimont, Jean-François, 74, 75
Blarenberghe family, 29
Blondel, Jacques-François, 24, **24**, **25**, 49, 51, 52, **52**, **53**, 55, **57**
boiserie. See paneling

Bone, Lesley, 8, 9
Bonnet, Xavier, 11, 12, 13, 26, 28, 29, 33n23, **71**, 93, 103
Borra, Giovanni Battista, **3**
Boulle, André-Charles, 36, 38
Boze, Joseph, 75
Brettingham, Matthew, the Elder, **3**
Brissac family, 66n23
Buck, Susan, 92–93

Cailleteau, Pierre, 25, 51
California Palace of the Legion of Honor, San Francisco: Louis XV Room in, 15n1; Louis XVI Room in, **18**, 31n1; Salon Doré acquired by, 3, 17, 21; Salon Doré's first installation (1962) at, 3–4, 17, **18**, 24, 77, 78, 88, 91, 114, **114**; Salon Doré's second installation (1995) at, **4**, **5**, 6, 19, 77, 78, 79, 88, 114, **114**; Salon Doré's third installation (2014) at, 4–9, 11–14, 19, 77–95, **100–101**, 115, **115**; seismic retrofitting of, 4, 114; Spanish palace ceiling displayed in, 2
canapés, 7, 11, 102, 103, 115
Capin, Claude-François, 54, 72, 73, 75
capitals of pilasters in the Salon Doré, 81–82
Carlhian, Parisian paneling dealer, 21
Carlhian Records, 21, 32n13
ceiling of the Salon Doré, 4, 6–7, 17, 91, 115; rosette in, 7, 17, **18**, 91
Chabot, duc de, 40, **40**
chairs. See armchairs; kneeling chairs; side chairs
chaises courantes, *volantes*, or *d'usage*. See side chairs
Chalgrin, Jean-François-Thérèse, **78**
chandeliers, 7, 13, 15n6, 28, 32n13, 35–36, 37, 57, 64, 77, 99, 102, 111, **111**
chandelles. See pilasters
Chanel, Pierre-Olivier, 13
Château de Bellevue, 107

Château de Chanteloup, 72
Château de Ménars, **41**
Château de Saint-Leu, 11, 103, 109
Châtillon, duc de, 25, 67n26
Châtillon, Louise-Emmanuelle de, 5, 25, 50, **50**
Cheverny, comte de, 45
Chevotet, Jean-Michel, **25**, **49**, **53**, **57**
chimneypieces, 9, 11, 28, 29, **31**, 33n29, 35, 37, 38, 57, 58, 61, 64, 79, 107
Choiseul, duc de, **29**, 45
Choiseul-Praslin, duc de, 38
Choiseul snuffbox, 29, **29**
Clermont-Tonnerre family, 66n23
clocks, 13, 28, 58, 61, 62, 63, 64, 65, 77, 98, 102, 103, 106, **106**
Coigny, duc de, 54
color, paint. See paint color
color schemes of furnishings in the Hôtel de La Trémoille (1790 inventory), 56, 60, 65–66
color schemes of furnishings in the Salon Doré, 8; at Hôtel de La Trémoille, 14, 28–29, 60, 70, **71**, 72; at Legion of Honor (2014), 12, 14, 115
comfortable seating, development of, 46–47
commodes, 9, 37, 38, 55, 60, 61, 64, 102
conservation of the Salon Doré, 7–9, 14, 77–95; doors, 88–89; mirror frames, 77–78, 82, 88; overdoor reliefs, 89–90; paint color, 92–93; paneling, 7–9, 77–88, 92, 95, 115
console tables, 7, 9, 11, **12**, 13, 14, 28, 37, 38, 58–59, 61, 97, 102, 103, 107, **107**, 115
Convent of the Annunciation, Paris, 51
Cooper-Hewitt, National Design Museum, New York, 12–13, 73
Corcoran Gallery of Art, Washington, DC, 11, 15n2, 77, **78**, 81
Croix, marquise de, 24, 112

Crown's *garde-meuble* (furniture repository), 73
curtains: in the Hôtel de La Trémoille (1790 inventory), 55, 56, 60, 61, 62, 63, 64, 65, 66; in the Salon Doré, 4, 12, 13, 14, 15n14, 28, 29, 32n13, 60, 70, 72, 73–74, **74**, 99

Daguerre, French art dealer, 54
Danloux, Henri-Pierre, **48**, **103**, 105
Darnault, François-Charles, 54
David-Weill Collection, Paris, 103, 109
Declercq Passementiers, **68**, **72**, 103
decorative art in the Salon Doré: at Hôtel de La Trémoille, 28, 30, 33n29, 53, 54, 57–58; at Legion of Honor (2014), 7–9, 14, 89–90
Decour decorating firm, 19, 114
Delafosse, Jean-Charles, 110
Delapoize, Pierre-Auguste, 4, 6, 28, 33n25, 53, 57, 67n28
Delarue, Charles, 72
Delaunay, Nicolas, **44**
Dell, Theodore, 111
Dequevauviller, François, **31**
de Young Museum, San Francisco, 1, 3, 32n6, 102
Diderot, Denis, 74
dimensions of the Salon Doré. *See* proportions of the Salon Doré
dishware, 36, 62–63
door cases of the Salon Doré: at Hôtel de La Trémoille, 30, 33n29; at Legion of Honor (2014), 6, 7, 78, 89
doors of the Salon Doré: at Hôtel d'Humières, 88; at Legion of Honor (1962), 88; at Legion of Honor (1995), 88; at Legion of Honor (2014), 6, 14, **84**, 88–89, **89**, **94**
doorways in the Salon Doré, at Kahn mansion, 6, 13, 21, 88
Dujardin, Paul, **50**
Dumégnil, Cécile de, 54
Duplessis, Joseph, 75
Duveen Brothers (New York art dealers), 17, 19, **20**, 21, 31n3, 79, **113**, 114

entablature in the Salon Doré, 90–91
expenditures, archival records of, at the Hôtel de La Trémoille, 28, 54–56, 58–64, 66n21, 67nn, 97–99

fauteuils. *See* armchairs
Fine Arts Museums of San Francisco, 3, 84, 111

firedogs, 28, 57, 61, 62, 63, 64, 65, 77, 97, 102, **110**, 110–11
fireplaces, **23**, 28, 39, 40, **40**, 42, **44**, 61, 62, 63, 64, 65, 77, 97, 98, 110
Fitz-James, duc de, 66n23
Fixon family, **2**, 8, 89
floor plan: of Hôtel de La Trémoille, **51**, **52**, **55**; of Hôtel d'Humières, **6**, **24**; of Hôtel du Châtelet, **30**; of Hôtel du Nivernais, **30**
Fowles, Edward, 21, 31n3, 32nn
France: Old Regime in, 35, 37, 46; Reign of Terror in, 27; Restoration in, 46; Revolution in, 13, 25, 27, 28, 33n25, 50, 112
Frederick III, prince of Salm-Kyrburg, 27
French & Company, 110, 111
Frénilly, baron de, 41–42, 42–43, 45–46
furniture in the Hôtel de La Trémoille (1790 inventory), 28–30, 54, 55, 56, 58–62, 63, 64, 65, 97–99
furniture in the Salon Doré: at Duveen Brothers showroom, 21; at Hôtel de La Trémoille, 28–30, 58–60; at Hôtel d'Humières, **6**, 23; at Legion of Honor (1962), 4; at Legion of Honor (2014), 7, 9, 11, 12–14, **107**, **108**, 108–9, **109**, 115. *See also* seating; tables

Gabriel, Ange-Jacques, 17, 114
gaming, 9, **16**, 30, **31**, 36, 40, 43, 44, 45, 56, 50
Gary Collection, 111
Genlis, comtesse de, 38, 40, 42, 43, 46
Getty Museum, Los Angeles, 2, 72
gilding in the Salon Doré: on ceiling rosette, 7, **18**; on chandelier, **111**; on doors, 88, **89**; on firedogs, 110; on furniture, 14, 15n9, 28, 58–59, 107, **107**, **108**, **109**; on mantel clock, 106, **106**; on mirror frames, 8, 30, 33n29, **86**; on paneling, 28, 30, 33n29, 57, 80–81, **81**, **82**, 83–87; on pilasters, 4, 30, 33n29; on torchères, 107, **107**; on vases, 105, **105**; on wall lights, 110, **110**
Gramont, duchesse de, 39

Harris, John, 4, 17, 114
Haussmann, Georges-Eugène, 4, 21, 24
Hearst, William Randolph, 111
Heil, Walter, 32n6
Héricourt, Nicolas, 54, 56
Heussée, French architect, 50
Hillingdon collection, London, 21, 32n6
Hôtel de Beauvau, Paris, **40**
Hôtel de Berny, Amiens, 72, 73

Hôtel de Béthune, Paris, 25, **25**, 49, **52**, **53**, **57**, 112
Hôtel de Châtillon, Paris, 25, **25**, 49, **52**, **53**, **57**, 112
Hôtel de Clermont, Paris, 77, **78**, 82
Hôtel de Crillon, Paris, 17, 19, 114
Hôtel de La Trémoille, rue de Vaugirard, Paris, 33n25, 50
Hôtel de La Trémoille, rue Saint-Dominique, Paris: *appartements de société* in, 52, 55–56; arrangement of rooms in, **51**, 51–53, **52**; artisans and servants employed at, 52, 54, 55, 56, 58, 65, 67; audience rooms (*salles du dais*) in, 26, 29, 52, 56, 65, 66; Blondel's architectural studies of, 24, **24**, 25, 51, 52, **52**; cabinetwork in, 60, 61, 62, 63, 64; Chevotet's drawings of, **25**, **49**, **53**, **57**; chimneypieces in, 57, 61, 64; color scheme of furnishings in, 56, 60, 65–66; Croix, marquise de, as owner of, 24, 112; curtains in, 55, 56, 60, 61, 62, 63, 64, 65, 66; decorative art at, 28, 30, 33n29, 53–54, 57–59; Delapoize's architectural renovations of, 4, 6, 28, 33n25, 53–54, 57; demolition of, 4, 112; dining room in, 52, 55; duchess's rooms in, 52–53, 54, 56–63; duke's rooms in, 53, 63–65; fireplaces in, 57, 61, 62, 63, 64, 65, 97, 98; floor plan of, **51**, **52**, **55**; fortepiano in, 64; furniture in, 28–30, 54, 55, 56, 58–62, 63, 64, 65, 97–99; garden of, **51**, 51, 57; installation of Salon Doré at, 4–5, 24, 28–30, 56–60, 112; inventory of Salon Doré at, 8, 12, 13–14, 28, 29, 30, 49, **59**, 60, 93, **96**, 97–99, 110; Lassurance as architect of, 25, 51; La Trémoille family as residents of, 24–28, 49–50, 66; library of, 53, 61–62, 66; lighting fixtures in, 57, 61, 62, 63, 64; Marescot, General, as resident of, 28; Ministry of War offices at, 28; Miromesnil, marquis de, as resident of, 49; mirrors in, 53, 55, 56, 57, 60, 61, 62, 63, 64, 65, 98; origination of Salon Doré at, 4–5, 24, 28, 112; paintings at, 53, 56, 61, 64; paneling in, 5, 24, **25**, 26, 53, 56, 57, 60, 62, 63, 65; records of expenditures at, 28, 54–56, 58–64, 66n21, 67nn; servants' quarters in, 52, 53, 55, 65; *trumeaux* (piers) in, 55, 56, 57, 60, 61, 63, 64, 65; upholstery in, 29, 54, 55, 56, 60, 61, 62, 63, 64, 69–75; Uzès, duchesse d', as owner of, 28; wall hangings in, 54, 56, 57; water closet in, 65
Hôtel de Luynes, Paris, **16**, **31**, **43**

Hôtel de Neuchâtel, Paris, 25, 112
Hôtel de Noailles, Paris, 36, 37, 47n6
Hôtel de Salm, Paris, 4, 14, 27, **27**, **50**, **69**
Hôtel de Tessé, Paris, **2**, 15nn2,14, 77, 89
Hôtel de Toulouse, Paris, 9, 37, 47n6, 103, 108
Hôtel d'Humières, Paris, 4, 5, **6**, 17, 21, **23**, 23–24, **24**, **50**, 82, 83, 88, 89, 90, 91, 112, **112**, 113, 114
Hôtel d'Orsay, 15n16
Hôtel du Châtelet, Paris, **30**
Hôtel du Nivernais, Paris, **30**
Hôtel d'Uzès, 15n16
Hôtel Grimod de La Reynière, Paris, 15n5, **58**
Hôtel Lambert, Paris, 51
Howe, Thomas Carr, 3, 32n3, 95n6
Hue, Armand Thomas, 49
Huyot, Nicolas, **2**

installations of the Salon Doré: at Duveen Brothers showroom, **20**, 21, 79, 113, **113**; at Hôtel de La Trémoille, 4–5, 24, 28–30, 56–60, 112; at Hôtel d'Humières, 4, 5, **6**, 21, **23**, 23–24, 82, 83, 89, 91, 112, 113, **113**; at Kahn mansion, 6, 13, 21, **22**, 79, 88, 90, 93, 113; at La Dolphine mansion, 17, 19, 78, 88, 114; at Legion of Honor (1962), 3–4, 17, **18**, 24, 77, 78, 88, 91, 114, **114**; at Legion of Honor (1995), 4, **5**, 6, 19, 77, 78, 79, 88, 114, **114**; at Legion of Honor (2014), 4–7, 11–14, 19, 77–95, **100–101**, 115, **115**
inventory (1790) of the Salon Doré, 8, 12, 13–14, 28, 29, 30, 49, **59**, 60, 93, **96**, 97–99, 110

Jacob, Georges, 9, 11, 103, 108, 109
Jefferson, Thomas, 27

Kahn, Otto, 21
Kahn mansion, New York, 6, 13, 21, **22**, 32n13, 79, 88, 90, 93, 113
Kammsetzer, Johann Christian, **58**
Kimball, Fiske, 2
Kisluk-Grosheide, Daniëlle, 15n14
kneeling chairs (*voyeuses*), 30, 44, 60

La Dolphine mansion, Hillsborough, California, 17, 19, **19**, 78, 88, 114
Lafrensen, Niclas, II, **31**
Lalonde, Richard de, 11, **12**, 107
lampas, 12, 63, 64, 65, 66, 70, **70**, **71**, 72, 74
La Pouplinière, Alexandre Leriche de, 43
Lassurance (Pierre Cailleteau), 25, 51

La Tour du Pin, marquise de, 44, 45
La Trémoille family, 5, 13–14, 24–28, **26**, 30, 33n21, 49–50, 54, 56, 66, **69**, 112. *See also* Hôtel de La Trémoille
Laval, Anne de, 27
Legion of Honor. *See* California Palace of the Legion of Honor
Lepaute brothers, 106
Le Vau, Louis, 51
lighting fixtures of the Salon Doré: at Hôtel de La Trémoille, 13, 28, 57; at Legion of Honor (1995), **5**, 7; at Legion of Honor (2014), 7, 15n6, 115. *See also* chandeliers; sconces; torchères; wall lights
lits à la turque, 61, 63
Loma Prieta earthquake, 107
Louis XIV, 9, 56
Louis XIV style, 31n1
Louis XV, 35
Louis XV Room at the Legion of Honor, 15n1
Louis XV style, 19
Louis XVI, 35, 49, 106, 107, 108
Louis XVI Room at the Legion of Honor, **18**, 31n1
Louis XVI style, 9, 24, 32n13, 107, 108, 109
Louvre museum, Paris, 106, 107
Love, emblem of, 8, **8**, 30, 89
Lowengard, Armand, 31n3
Luxembourg, Marshal de, wife of, 38, 39–40
Luynes, duchesse de, 67n23
Lyon: Musée Historique des Tissus in, 12, 14, 70, **71**, 72; silk manufacturers in, 70, 103

Mallet, Jean-Baptiste, **43**
maquette (model) of the Salon Doré, 19, **20**, 21, 32n6
Marchand, Richard, **22**
Marescot, General, 28
Marie-Antoinette, 25
Marie-Maximilienne, princess of Salm-Kyrburg, 27, 112
Marigny, marquis de, **41**, 47n9, 54
Mazarin, duchesse de, 9, **10**, 66n23
Metropolitan Museum of Art, New York, 2, 7, 13, 15n2, 21, 77, 89
Michau, Jean-Baptiste-Nicolas, 50
Mills, Charles, 32n9
minimalism in museum design, 1, 4
Miromesnil, marquis de, 49
mirror frames in the Salon Doré, **8**, 30, 33n29, 77–78, 82, **83**, **86**, 88, 110
mirrors in Hôtel de La Trémoille (1790

inventory), 53, 55, 56, 57, 60, 61, 62, 63, 64, 65, 98
mirrors in the Salon Doré: at Hôtel de La Trémoille, 13, 28, 30, 33n27, 57; at Legion of Honor (2014), 6, **8**, 13, 78, 103
Mobilier National, Paris, 70
mobiliers meublantes, 9, 14, 108
Morovic, Natasa, 7, **81**, 84, **85**
Musée des Arts Décoratifs, Paris, 12
Musée Historique des Tissus, Lyon, 12, 14, 70, **71**, 72
Museum of Fine Arts, Boston, 12

Neoclassicism, 3–4, 9, 11, 27, 53, 57, 107, 108, 109
Norfolk House Music Room, London, 2, **3**

Orléans, duchesse d', 11, 109
Ossun, marquis d', **75**
Ouziel, Fabrice, 15n7
overdoors, **2**, 8, 30, 53, 61, 63, 64, 89–90, **91**

paint color in the Salon Doré, 8–9, 13, 14, 28, 57, 92–93
Palace of the Legion of Honor. *See* California Palace of the Legion of Honor
Palais Royal, Paris, 37
Palmstedt, Erik, 30, **30**
paneling (*boiserie*) of the Salon Doré, conservation of: in the past, 77, 82–84; in the present, 7–9, 77–88, 92, 95
paneling (*boiserie*) of the Salon Doré, installations of, 112; at Duveen Brothers showroom, 21, 113; at Hôtel de La Trémoille, 5, 24, **25**, 26, 57; at Hôtel d'Humières, **6**, 23, 24, 89, 112; at Kahn mansion, 21, 113; at La Dolphine mansion, 17, 88, 114; at Legion of Honor (1962), 3–4, 17, 19, 77; at Legion of Honor (1995), 4, **5**, 19, 77, 114, **114**; at Legion of Honor (2014), 11, 14, 19, 115
Paris, urban renewal in, 4, 21, 23, 24
parquetry in the Salon Doré, 115; in ceiling, **5**; in floor, 4, **5**, 6, 7, 14, 17, **18**; in mirror casings, 33n29, **76**, 82, **83**
Penthièvre, duc de, 9, 11, 108
Périer, Guillaume, 9, 103, 108
period rooms, museum installations of, 1–3
Pernon, Camille, 70
Philadelphia Museum of Art, 2
pilasters of the Salon Doré: at Hôtel de La

Trémoille, 30, 33n29, 58; at Legion of Honor (2014), 4, 6, 78, **82**. *See also* capitals
Pitoin, Claude-Jean, 111
Pons, Bruno, 4, 5, 7, 24, 30, 33n21
porcelain, 28, 32n9, 37, 38, 58, 60, 62–63, 64, 65, 77, 97, 105, **105, 106**, 110
Poussin, Charles-Henry, 54
proportions of the Salon Doré, 5–6, **6**, 21, 24, 114, 115
provenance of the Salon Doré, 4, 5, 17, 19, 24, 28, 30, 31n2, 114
Provence, comte de, 75

reception rooms (*salons de compagnie*), 7, 30, 35–37, 44, 57, 102, 112
Remy, Pierre, 35–36
Rheem, Richard, 3, 17, 19, 21, 32n6, 88, 114
Richelieu, duc de, 66n23
Rohan-Rohan, duc de, 66n23
rooms, in French mansions: antechambers, 26, 29, 35, 36, 42, 44, 45, 46, 52, 55, 56, **57**, 65; *appartements de société*, 26, 28, 30, 35, 51–52, 55–56, 61; audience rooms (*salles du dais*), **2**, 26, 29, 52, 56, 60, 63, 65, 66; bedchambers, 26, 35, 37, 52, 54, 56, 60–61, 63–64, 65; boudoirs, 37, 53, 54, 62–63, 66; dining rooms, 19, 36, 42, 46, 52, 55, 66, 67n23; dressing rooms, 9, 37, 53, 54, 63, 65; hierarchical arrangement of, 35–37, 55, 56, 65; libraries, 37, 53, 61–62, 63, 66; private rooms, 37, **44**, 52–53, 102; reception rooms, 7, 30, 35–37, 44, 57, 102, 112; servants' quarters, 36, 52, 53, 55, 65; water closets, 65. *See also* salons
Rorimer, James, 21
Rosebery Collection, Mentmore, England, 109
rosettes, 33n29, 58, 59; and ceiling rosette in the Salon Doré, 7, 17, **18**, 91
Rothschild mansion, Mentmore, England, 103, 109
Roubo, André-Jacob, **80**
Royer family, French artisans, 28, 54, 58

salles du dais. See audience rooms
Salm, prince de, **69**
salons, in French mansions: cabinetwork in, 37; chandeliers in, 35, 37; formal bedchambers adjacent to, 37; furnishing of, 7, 9, 11, 13, 30, 35, 37, 38, 42, 46, 60, 102–103; gaming in, **16**, **31**, 43–44; hierarchical arrangement of, 35–37; impersonal aspect of, 37–38; musical performances in, 43;

rectangular vs. square configuration of, 5, 15n5; social status signified by, 37, 38. *See also* reception rooms (*salons de compagnie*)
Sanchez-Goodwillie, Erika, 93
sconces, **3**, 23, 57, 58, 61, 62, 63, 64
Scott, John Murray, 111
seating arrangements, **29, 30, 31,** 38–42, **39, 40, 41, 43,** 44
seating in the Salon Doré: at Hôtel de La Trémoille, 13, 28–30, 59–60; at Legion of Honor (2014), 9, 11, 102–103. *See also* armchairs; kneeling chairs; side chairs; sofas
Sené, French artisan, 11, 28, 54, 58
Sèvres vases, 14, 105, **105, 106**
side chairs in the Hôtel de La Trémoille (1790 inventory), 55, 56, 59, 61, 62, 63, 64, 65, 74, 98, 99
side chairs in the Salon Doré: at Hôtel de La Trémoille, 13, 29, 59–60; at Legion of Honor (2014), 7, 9, 11, 103, **108,** 109, **109,** 115
sièges meublants (formal seats), 38
silk lampas. *See* lampas
Skurman, Andrew, 7, **115**
social life of French upper class, architectural design for, 29–30, 35–47; aristocratic compared to bourgeois, 36, 38; and dining, 36, 43, 44–46, 52; and gaming, **16**, 30, **31**, 40, 43–44, 56, 60; and heating, 36, 39–40, 42, 46, 52; and hierarchical arrangement of rooms, 35–37; and married couples' separate rooms, 26, 36; and private rooms, 37, **44**, 52–53; and reception rooms, 30, 35–37, 44, 57, 102, 112; and seating arrangements, **29,** 38–42, **39, 40, 43,** 44
sofas, 9, 11, 14, 15n9, 37, 38, 60, 62, 64, 72, 75, 99, 102, 108. See also *canapés*
square configuration of the Salon Doré, 5–6, **6**, 15n5, 21, 24, 114, 115
Staffe, baronne, 42
Steinitz, Benjamin, 7
Stenhouse, J. Armstrong, 21
Swan suite at Museum of Fine Arts, Boston, 12

tables, 9, 36, 43, 46, 54, 55, 60, 61, 62, 65; breakfast, 60, 64, 99; dining, 36, 45, 46; dressing, 63; gaming, 9, 30, 36, 43–44, 56, 60; night, 54, 60, 65; writing, 36. *See also* console tables
Tarente family, 5, 25, 27, 28, 30, 33nn21,23, 49–50, **50**, 54, 57

Tassinari & Chatel textile firm, 70, **71**, 103
textiles in the Salon Doré, 11, 12, 14, 60, 103. *See also* curtains; lampas; upholstery; wall hangings
Thélusson, madame de, 54, 66n18
Thorpe, Adam, 8, **8**, 87, **87**
torchères, 7, 14, 77, 102, 107, **107**
trictrac, 9, 30, **31**, 45, 56
trophies, carved, **2**, 4, 6, 7–8, **8**, 30, 78, 80, 83, **86**, 87
Troy, Jean François de, 39, **39**
trumeaux (piers), 55, 56, 57, 60, 61, 62, 63, 64, 65

upholstery in the Hôtel de La Trémoille (1790 inventory), 29, 54, 55, 56, 60, 61, 62, 63, 64, 69–75, 98, 99
upholstery in the Salon Doré, 69–75, 103; color scheme of, 14, 28, 29, 60, 70, 72, 115; fabrics used in, 12, 60, 70, **70, 71,** 72, 103, 115; and padding styles, 74–75, **75**; and trimmings, 72, **72**, 103; and window embellishments, **73**, 73–74, **74**
Utrecht velvet, 29, 55, 56, 60, 64, 65, 98, 99

Vanderbilt mansion, New York, 110
van Loo, César, **75**
vases, 11, 13, 14, 23, 28, 38, 57–58, 59, 62, 63, 64, 65, 77, 97, 102, 105, **105, 106**; garnitures of, 13, 14, 28, 97, 102, 105, **105**, 110
Verlet, Pierre, 7
Versailles, 9, 37, 40, 45, 50, **52**
Victoria and Albert Museum, London, 1, 2, **3**
Vitet, Antoine, 54, 55, 56, 59, 60, 61, 62, 63, 64, 67
voyeuses. See kneeling chairs

Waddesdon Manor, England, 24
Wallace Collection, London, 21, 111
wall hangings, 36, 37, 38, 54, 57
wall lights, 7, 13, 15n6, 28, 32n13, 35, 57, 97, 98, 102, 110, **110**
Wellington, Winfield Scott, 17, **18**, 19, 24, 31n2, 90, 92, 95n6, 114
Whale, Winifred Stephens, 25
windows of the Salon Doré: at Hôtel d'Humières, 24; at Legion of Honor (1962), 24; at Legion of Honor (2014), 6, 14, 107, 115, **115**
Wrightsman rooms, at Metropolitan Museum of Art, New York, 2, 7, 15n14

Published by the Fine Arts Museums of San Francisco on the occasion of the renovation and conservation of the Salon Doré from the Hôtel de La Trémoille at the Legion of Honor.

The catalogue is published with the assistance of the European Decorative Arts Council (EDAC) and the Andrew W. Mellon Foundation Endowment for Publications.

Fine Arts Museums of San Francisco
Golden Gate Park
50 Hagiwara Tea Garden Drive
San Francisco, CA 94118-4502
www.famsf.org

MAJOR PATRONS
Cynthia Fry Gunn and John A. Gunn

CORPORATE SPONSOR
Breguet

Produced through the Publications Department of the Fine Arts Museums of San Francisco
Leslie Dutcher, *Director of Publications*
Laura Harger, *Editor*
Danica Michels Hodge, *Editor*

Wilsted & Taylor Publishing Services
Project management: Christine Taylor
Art management: Jennifer Uhlich
Copy editor: Melody Lacina
Design and composition: Yvonne Tsang
Color separations and illustrations: Evan Winslow Smith

French translations by Rose Vekony

Printed in Canada by Friesens Corporation, Altona, Manitoba

© 2014 Fine Arts Museums of San Francisco

All rights reserved. No part of this publication may be reproduced, stored in a retrieval system, or transmitted in any form or by any means, electronic, mechanical, photocopying, recording, or otherwise, without prior written consent of the publishers.

Every effort has been made to identify the rightful copyright holders of material not specifically commissioned for use in this publication and to secure permission, where applicable, for reuse of all such material. Credit, if and as available, has been provided for all borrowed material either on the page, on the copyright page, or in the acknowledgments or picture credit section of the book. Errors or omissions in credit citations or failure to obtain permission if required by copyright law have been either unavoidable or unintentional. The authors and the publisher welcome any information that would allow them to correct future reprints.

Library of Congress Cataloging-in-Publication Data

Fine Arts Museums of San Francisco.
  The Salon Doré from the Hôtel de La Trémoille / Martin Chapman ; with Alexandre Pradère, Xavier Bonnet, Lesley Bone, Maria Santangelo.
    pages cm
  Includes bibliographical references.
  ISBN 978-0-88401-142-2
  1. Salon Doré (Legion of Honor, San Francisco, Calif.). 2. Architectural woodwork—France—Paris. 3. Decoration and ornament—France—Neoclassicism. 4. Architectural woodwork—Conservation and restoration—California—San Francisco. I. Chapman, Martin (Curator). II. Chapman, Martin (Curator), author. History of the Salon. III. Title.
  NA3900.F56 2014
  727'.70979461—dc23   2013045261

Page 16: François Dequevauviller, *L'assemblé au salon* (*Gathering in a Salon*), 1783 (detail of fig. 23). Page 34: Jean François de Troy, *The Reading from Molière*, ca. 1728 (detail of fig. 24). Page 48: Henri-Pierre Danloux, *The Baron de Besenval in His Salon de Compagnie*, 1791 (detail of fig. 67). Page 68: Contemporary silk reweaving by Tassinari & Chatel, with *passementerie* by Declercq (fig. 46). Page 76: Mirror casing, ca. 1781 (detail of fig. 56). Page 96: Page from the 1790 inventory of the Hôtel de La Trémoille in the Archives Nationales, Paris; photo courtesy Xavier Bonnet. Page 104: Mantel clock, ca. 1780 (detail of cat. no. 3), © Fine Arts Museums of San Francisco.

PHOTOGRAPHY CREDITS
COVER: Randy Dodson, © Fine Arts Museums of San Francisco.
FRONT MATTER: Pages ii–iii: Randy Dodson, © Fine Arts Museums of San Francisco. Pages iv, vi, viii, xii: Henrik Kam, © Fine Arts Museums of San Francisco.
FIGURE ILLUSTRATIONS: 1, 52: image copyright © The Metropolitan Museum of Art. Image source: Art Resource, NY. 2, 6, 7: copyright © Victoria and Albert Museum, London / V&A Images—All rights reserved. 3, 5, 11, 23, 28, 51, 54, 55, 56, 57, 59, 60, 62, 65, 66, 71: Randy Dodson, © Fine Arts Museums of San Francisco. 4, 15, 68: courtesy Société d'histoire et d'archéologie du VIIe arrondissement de Paris. 8, 70: © Fine Arts Museums of San Francisco. 9: courtesy Environmental Design Archives, University of California, Berkeley. 10: Getty Images. 12, 69: Duveen Brothers library, The Clark Institute; courtesy Getty Research Institute. 14: courtesy House Committee, Convent of the Sacred Heart, New York. 16: Kyoto University Library. 17, 29, 34, 36: © Beaux-Arts de Paris, Dist. RMN-Grand Palais / Art Resource, NY. 18: University of California, Berkeley Library. 19: Archives Charmet / The Bridgeman Art Library. 20: Cria Images. 21, 22: Royal Swedish Academy of Fine Arts, photos by Thomas Wryeson. 24: The Bridgeman Art Library. 25, 26, 27: courtesy Alexandre Pradère. 30: General Research Division, The New York Public Library, Astor, Lenox and Tilden Foundations. 32: courtesy Archives Nationales, Paris. 33: photo by Gérard Blot, © RMN-Grand Palais / Art Resource, NY. 37: University of Warsaw Library, photo by Krystyna Dabrowska. 38, 39, 45, 46, 48: courtesy Xavier Bonnet and Atelier Saint-Louis. 40: Musée national de la Légion d'honneur et des ordres de chevalerie, Paris. Photograph by ECPAD. 41: courtesy Tassinari & Chatel. 42, 43: courtesy Martin Chapman. 44: courtesy Musée Historique des Tissus, Lyon. 47: Cooper-Hewitt, National Design Museum, Smithsonian Institution / Art Resource, NY; photo by Matt Flynn. 49: courtesy National Gallery of Art, Washington, DC. 50: Corcoran Gallery of Art, Washington, DC. 53, 63, 64: Conservation Department, © Fine Arts Museums of San Francisco. 58, 61: Henrik Kam, © Fine Arts Museums of San Francisco. 67: © National Gallery, London / Art Resource, NY. 72, 73: courtesy Andrew Skurman Architects.
GALLERY: Henrik Kam, © Fine Arts Museums of San Francisco.
CATALOGUE ILLUSTRATIONS: 1, 2, 3, 4, 5, 9, 10, 11: © Fine Arts Museums of San Francisco. 6, 7, 8: courtesy Xavier Bonnet and Atelier Saint-Louis. 12: Henrik Kam, © Fine Arts Museums of San Francisco.